The Assertiveness Guide for Women

Learn to Set Boundaries and Be Assertive with a Strong Personality - Includes Tips to Effectively Communication with Others

Margaret Douglas

©Copyright 2021 Margaret Douglas All rights reserved

The content contained within this book may not be reproduced, duplicated, or transmitted without direct written permission from the author or the publisher.

Under no circumstances will any blame or legal responsibility be held against the publisher, or author, for any damages, reparation, or monetary loss due to the information contained within this book, either directly or indirectly.

Legal Notice

This book is copyright protected. This book is only for personal use. You cannot amend, distribute, sell, use, quote or paraphrase any part, or the content within this book, without the consent of the author-publisher.

Disclaimer Notice

Please note the information contained within this document is for educational and entertainment purposes only. All effort has been executed to present accurate, up to date, and reliable, complete information. No warranties of any kind are declared or implied. Readers acknowledge that the author is not engaging in the rendering of legal, financial, medical, or professional advice.

TABLE OF CONTENTS

Introduction 5

Chapter 1 What does it Mean to be Assertive? 9

Chapter 2 Developing Assertiveness 14

Chapter 3 Factors that Prevent you from Being Assertive 19

Chapter 4 Advantages of Being Assertive 27

Chapter 5 Assertive Communication 30

Chapter 6 Assertiveness for Women 48

Chapter 7 Different Communication Styles 53

Chapter 8 People-pleasing Mindset 57

Chapter 9 Build your Confidence 65

Chapter 10 Setting Boundaries 70

Chapter 11 Active Listening 78

Chapter 12 Saying No is your Right 82

Chapter 13 The Power of Positive Language 88

Chapter 14 Speaking your Truth, Communicating your Needs 92

Chapter 15 Verbal and Non-Verbal Language 100

Chapter 16 Getting to Know Yourself 104

Chapter 17 Emotional Intelligence 115

Chapter 18 Handling Negative Comments 118

Chapter 19 Stop Apologizing All the Time 124

Chapter 20 Stress and Anxiety Management 130

Chapter 21 Anger Management 136

Chapter 22 Be Assertive 145

Chapter 23 What an Assertive Person is Like 150

Chapter 24 When Nothing is Working 153

Chapter 25 Training your Mind to Become Assertive 158

Conclusion 164

Introduction

The ability to express your feelings, thoughts, convictions, desires, needs, wishes, and opinions while staying respectful of the rights of others is referred to as assertiveness. It's a skill that can be developed. It takes bravery to be yourself and remove the masks that others have placed on you. You accept the risk of being involved, visible, unique, thoughtful, flawed, and vulnerable while keeping consistent in your ideas and rights. You take the risk of becoming unique. You also have confidence in your abilities to deal with any issues that develop as a result of your perseverance.

Assertiveness does not entail any type of aggressiveness. It's a proclamation of one's power to dominate and control another person. It can be a cold, deliberate attack designed to inflict pain, wound, intimidate, defeat, dominate, or humiliate the other individual or group. Excessive retribution or the release of multiple repressed and unacknowledged strong emotions can also lead to aggressive behavior. Aggressive communication is defined as prioritizing one's own desires and attempting to communicate or achieve one's goals by infringing on the rights and needs of others. You can persuade someone to give you what you want without their consent by being aggressive.

A confrontational voice has a stiff and chilly tone, a caustic and loud tone, and a threatening tone and delivery. Frequent interpretation can wreak havoc on one's capacity to keep conversational control. Just a few of the adjectives that spring to me include despising, cool, judging, sponsoring, repulsive, blunt, and foolish. They can also be deceptive and menacing. During an attack, the body's nonverbal communication is a source of concern. Personal space invasion, glaring, clinched fists, and teeth, pointing fingers, and other actions are all impacted.

This communication strategy may be able to provide you with the results you seek in the short term. When emotional development is allowed to flourish and external demands are restrained, a sense of power, control, and relief can be felt. Loss of links and social isolation; a persistent need to justify oneself; embarrassment; shame; low self-esteem; and an increased fear of confrontation are some of the long-term repercussions.

Passive communication is not the same as forceful communication. Passive communication's purpose is to avoid controversy at all costs, even if it means prioritizing one's own interests. Crowds, unreasonable requests, frustrations, refraining from criticizing or despising others, and feeling committed to resolving all concerns as if they were your own are just a few instances of how passive communication can be used.

When you communicate passively, you put others' wants and expectations ahead of your own desires, thoughts, and feelings, and vice versa. In other words, you're giving someone else control of your life. If one is unable to express one's own desires, others may abuse and exploit one's rights. Furthermore, it causes you to miss out on chances and causes others to overlook you, all of which can be detrimental to your self-esteem. Passive communicators generally whisper and speak in unison because they are often fearful of drawing attention to themselves. Apologies, divulging information, excuses, seeking authorization, and even self-disclaimers are all prevalent linguistic signals in today's world. Nonverbal communication includes fidgeting, avoiding eye contact, looking down and attempting to communicate, as well as a tense body position. When you are in danger or when the costs of self-expression outweigh the advantages, passive communication can be quite valuable.

The passive aggressive way of communication combines components of the previous two modes of communication. When you are outraged and communicate strongly, you feel driven to strike at the source of your annoyance or threat, whereas when you are hesitant to express your anger and reject others, you express yourself silently. By utilizing the passive aggressive method, you are seeking to conceal your anger and hatred while evading responsibility for your hostile behavior. Passive and aggressive communication can result from feelings of powerlessness, or rage, but they can also result from an inability to deal directly with the source of resentment, whether genuine or imagined. Recognizing and grasping one's own rage can be misunderstood as a threat to one's own well-being and hence branded as disappointment, frustration, or anything along those lines.

There are no audible signs of annoyance, despite the fact that the eyes are constantly roaming, and the lips are firmly pursed. Emotions and thoughts do not always match up with facial expressions. The rest of the world, for example, will smile at you regardless of how down you are. When the body is closed and the body language is neutral, anger and wrath may be less intense (a nervous laugh, raised eyebrows or crooked smile etc.). Sarcasm, selective forgetfulness, silent treatment, late mouthing, badly executing tasks, telling beneath the rib jokes, purposeful deterrence, and disturbing a plan are all examples of passive hostile behavior.

Consider a spectrum with two poles: aggressive and passive, with assertiveness in the center. To be forceful, one must first grasp one's own identity and role in society. You will not be able to establish yourself until you are aware of your own emotions, thoughts, desires, and wants. Being aware of your social environment is essential because it allows you to understand, grasp, and respect the wants and desires of others. With social awareness, you can forecast and judge how others will react to your affirmation, as well as psychologically prepare for the implications of your decisions and actions.

You'll need confidence, which comes with practice, to put your own demands on an equal basis with those of others. Assertiveness is defined as the capacity to speak up without annoyance, interruption, or criticism of others. It is necessary to set boundaries while remaining accepting and sympathetic. Being self-assured means making a conscious decision to express oneself and live in a certain way. Even in challenging situations, assertive communication involves the clear, honest, and concise expression of negative and positive emotions. The tone is assured, but also calm, caring, and sincere. It represents belonging and trust. Observations I make when looking for other points of view, needs, and compassion are typically included in the voice material. Body language communicates kindness, reassurance, openness, and comfort. Assertiveness is defined by the need to take responsibility for one's reactions and actions. Assertive behavior is employed to solve problems and achieve goals that benefit all parties concerned. It makes a deliberate effort to repress and divert fury and irritation.

Life's challenges present us with a wide range of scenarios, each of which may need a unique communication strategy and style. If you know how to communicate more aggressively, you may choose when, how, and when not to communicate.

Chapter 1
What does it Mean to be Assertive?

In recent years, the idea of assertiveness, which pertains to social skills, has gained popularity in clinical psychology and psychotherapy, and studies aiming at discovering and developing effective methods for fostering and strengthening assertiveness have increased in number. The term "assertiveness" derives from the Latin word "asserere," which means "to say," and refers to the act of affirming, "saying," and expressing one's opinions and emotional experiences in a safe and respectful manner.

According to Sanavio, affirmation is the ability to assert one's rights while also respecting the rights of others, which may be accomplished through rational and unambiguous verbal and nonverbal communication. Authors such as Wolpe, Salter, and Lazarus addressed it for the first time in history, even within the confines of their therapeutic profession. The majority of assertiveness training approaches are based on Wolpe's teachings, with some Salter's writings tossed in for good measure.

Conditioning Reflex Therapy, a study of Pavlov's theories released in 1949, is widely recognized as the world's first attempt to exhibit forceful behavior features. Salter believes that if a youngster is constantly chastised for specific areas of his social behavior, he would learn to limit that behavior and have an inhibited personality. As a result, Salter advocates for the use of coercive tactics in psychotherapy in certain circumstances.

He assigned tasks that focused on both verbal and nonverbal behavior, with the latter being more important: In fact, the use of a language capable of expressing any emotion is discovered, and this teaches the individual to express their emotion verbally; the use of a face mimic language, or facial movements associated with emotions, in order to express emotional statements with the face in a manner consistent with the oral context; and the use of a face mimic language, or facial movements associated with emotions, in order to express emotional statements with the face in a manner consistent with the oral context.

Even if you disagree, you can learn to express yourself fearlessly, to use the pronoun "I" instead of impersonal judgments, to accept compliments, to respect oneself, to be spontaneous, and to a variety of other abilities.

J. Wolpe coined the term "external manifestation of all other emotions" in 1959 to refer to the external manifestation of all other emotions other than anxiety: that is, Wolpe does not refer to an inhibited subject, but rather to someone who is unsure how to behave in a given situation, not necessarily as a result of aversive conditioning, but because, for example, he has never learned to swim.

JLMoreno and G. Kelly are two other authors who contributed significantly to the development of modern aggressive training techniques, albeit in different ways. Moreno, on the other hand, is widely regarded as the inventor of psychodrama, a technique for establishing attitudes and conflicts that is very similar to Wolpe's approach of 'playing a role,' one of his primary assertive strategies, though psychodrama is generally intended to promote catharsis and reflection.

G. Kelly offers a more nuanced approach to the concept of "fixed role," claiming that the individual emerges as a person free of the fears and feelings of inadequacy that have kept him in his habitual posture. This strategy is similar to aggressive training's repeated methods in several ways.

In contrast, Lazarus (1971) has expanded the role-playing process by emphasizing the need of presenting alternate behavior on the scene until tension is relieved. Bandura follows a similar line of thought, emphasizing the importance of explicit modeling in the process of developing new habits. While there are some differences among scholars who have studied assertiveness in the past and present, certain characteristics of this behavior can be identified: first and foremost, assertiveness entails the ability to defend one's rights, which includes the ability to say "no" or express one's own opinion, even if it differs from others.

Assertiveness is demonstrated by the capacity to initiate, sustain, and complete social contacts, as well as the ability to explain one's feelings, both good and negative, in a clear and straightforward manner. It can also be used to resolve conflicts and meet individual needs, such as asking for favors and making requests, demonstrating the ability to actively resist the pressures and effects of individuals or groups while remaining true to one's own values and viewpoints, and demonstrating the ability to actively resist the pressures and effects of individuals or groups while remaining true to one's own values and viewpoints.

It's critical to separate affirmativeness from two other types of behavior: aggression and passivity. If a person can only have these two kinds of interactions, he or she will become unbalanced, reacting aggressively at times and passively at others. While the emotional, cognitive, and expressive components must undoubtedly be tailored to the individual's current circumstances, expectations, and objectives, assertiveness must never devolve into infractions or condescending behavior that is not contrasted with the other. When it comes to relationships, the assertive style does not intend to cause conflict with others, but it can assist in achieving a favorable outcome by bringing opposing ideas together.

To be clear, the cultural context of belonging has a big impact on the definitions of these behaviors since it sets the social rules that must be observed and, as a result, the acceptability or not of a particular activity. The notion of choice is a crucial consideration when distinguishing between distinct modalities. In other words, assertive behavior is the consequence of deliberate intent: an assertive person chooses the behavior; a passive or aggressive person, on the other hand, is a victim of the behavior; it responds rather than acts in some respects.

To achieve one's goals, confidence entails accepting responsibility for one's actions, successfully communicating one's sentiments, and rejecting ineffective engagement strategies. To be forceful, one must not be pushed or frightened into expressing one's opinion. It is defined by the capacity to choose the best media for each particular relationship. Affirmation can also be viewed as a point of equilibrium between passive and active modes of communication. With a communication strategy that prioritizes communication, an individual can share his or her thoughts and emotional feelings, as well as commit to coping with difficult events and obstacles in a positive manner. The assertive answer cannot be preset; rather, it must be examined in the context of the social environment, and it is a process of communication improvement that is ongoing. As a result, assertive behavior does not bridge the gap between aggressive and passive behavior; rather, assertive communication attempts to eliminate aggressive and passive characteristics from communication. Assertiveness is a communication style that blends social skills, emotions, and logic while being true to one's own individuality. The neurovegetative factor, which is in charge of emotions, the voluntary motor, which is in charge of gestures and actions, and the cortical-cognitive element, which is in charge of verbalization and processing, all play a role during this integration. Because of their interdependence, strengthening assertiveness entails treating each of these three personality components separately. It is vital to comprehend not only confidence-building tactics, but also to cultivate new habits and teach them about their senses and emotions. Sentimental education is the process of being more aware of one's emotional environment.

As a philosophical framework, assertiveness refers to the order that everyone creates in their lives when they are more critical of themselves and purposeful in their interactions with others. This strategy creates a proactive and intelligent collaboration based on an accurate assessment of the situation and the tools to identify the most appropriate solution for the present challenge. The structure is based on the concept of liberty, which is described as the ability to be free of the harmful influences of one's surroundings. This entails becoming acquainted with oneself and one's personality, as well as learning about assertive rights theory (which includes the concept of reciprocity, which states that others recognize the same right to share one's desires and beliefs, as well as to pursue one's own goals) (this includes the idea of reciprocity, the same right for the communication of desires and beliefs and for the pursuit of individual aims is recognized also by others).

The second form of affirmability is the ability to convey oneself in a more sophisticated and effective manner, which translates to inadequate nonverbal and vocal communication skills, as well as overall social inadequacies. L. Philhps (1968) defines this aspect as "the extent to which an individual may communicate with others in a fair manner and without prejudice to similar rights, in the form of a free and open discourse" in order to meet rights and needs, as well as reasons and obligations. As a result, the self-serving personality is able to express sentiments, thoughts, wishes, and personal perspectives in a clear and technically successful manner, minimizing tension, discomfort, and animosity to a higher level than previously. This communication of communication contrasts with passive and aggressive ways.

Chapter 2
Developing Assertiveness

You may have overheard someone say, "The price to pay is a nice one." Our gratifications could be quite costly. We have the opportunity to spend the majority of our life putting others' needs ahead of our own. Our relationships frequently fall short of our expectations due to our inability to adequately convey ourselves.

Being empathetic may result in frustration if unforeseen repercussions occur. Even though they have hurt our feelings, some of us may be friendly to others out of concern for their feelings. Because we are agreeable, our views and desires are virtually always ignored or minimized in social circumstances. Being pleasant at work can prevent us from confronting people about their inappropriate behavior, which would call attention to the issue.

We, on the other hand, enjoy looking well! It all comes down to who we are and what we believe in, and that is a large part of it. You don't have to give up your lovely personality to learn how to say no to people. Our goal is to develop our assertiveness so that we can stop others from doing things with which we disagree or that are contrary to our ideals. It is not to allow anyone to anger or insult us. It is possible to be assertive while also being a kind person, meaning that we can be pleasant within specific limits.

Aggression is not synonymous with assertiveness.

You don't have to be aggressive to draw attention to your presence. Those who lack the skills to establish themselves and are driven by an aggressive desire to dominate others will face opposition. They adopt the bully character, whether on deliberately or not, in order to frighten and control others in order to attain their aims. A person's ambition to win stems from his or her desire to be aggressive. It is not our obligation to exert power upon these individuals. We will instead learn to be assertive without feeling obligated to be aggressive or domineering.

What are some of the benefits of assertiveness?

Because we are so focused on how others see us, it is easy to overlook the benefits of assertive behavior. As a starting point for enhancing communication skills, assertiveness is a great tool. When a conversation is conducted successfully, both sides profit and are not hurt.

When disputes are resolved amicably, there is far less stress and the creation of a negative atmosphere. This is especially true in the workplace, where problems must be resolved quickly to avoid harming the productivity of other employees or team members.Being assertive guarantees that you are taken seriously by others. It allows you to express yourself without fear of repercussions from others. This demonstrates to others that you are a trustworthy individual who goes above and beyond to earn the trust of others.

How to Increase Your Self-Assertion

Being assertive requires power and confidence. While it is not always easy to see things from another person's perspective, it is occasionally important. Consider the following scenario: one of your buddies is entirely uninterested in your weekend plans. Finding the line between assertive and aggressive behavior is more challenging than learning to be assertive through tried-and-true methods.

Assistive Techniques to Improve Your Assertiveness

To begin, determine exactly what you want. If you are unsure of the purpose of your assertive discussion, it will be difficult to deliver your message successfully. Rather than establishing a list of topics to debate about, it is preferable to focus on a single topic. If you don't like being touched, you should make a change. Your conversation will center on someone who takes an unusually long time.

Second, address your audience in the first person, paying special attention to adverbs that are frequently used.

Remember when we were learning how to deal with intruders and how crucial it was to communicate using the pronoun "I"? Instead of generalizing, sentences like "I do not feel appreciated in this setting" express specifically how you feel to the other person. Furthermore, using the term "you" followed by an insult is prohibited, as this will just intensify the problem.

In your writing, avoid using the words "always" and "never." Examine the distinctions between these two phrases: You've never thought twice about me.

When you express your thoughts clearly in the first line, the second phrase personalizes them and drives the other person to defend themselves, but the underlying issue stays hidden within your own feelings.

Remind yourself of the purpose of the practice.

Another reason to choose the appropriate wording is to avoid misunderstandings. We want the other person to realize how their behaviors affect our life when we assert ourselves. It is unconcerned about your human identity. It doesn't matter if they aren't the nicest person in the globe or the love of your life.

When the discourse is focused on the behavior rather than the person, an emotional and futile defensive reaction is less likely to arise.

As you read, keep the three Cs' assertiveness in mind.

Your message is succinct and well-thought-out. We appreciate your generosity. Throughout the conversation, you keep a calm, composed approach. It's well worth your time to plan out what you're going to say ahead of time so that your assertiveness incorporates all three of these qualities.

We use aggressive language when we say, "This isn't going to work," rather than assertive language like, "I believe we can view things differently." This implies that you will continue to listen and value what people have to say, but you will also be able to ask open-ended questions, which fosters rather than disrupts conversation, which is what assertiveness all about is.

Nonverbal behaviors such as erect posture, a clear, loud voice, and eye contact should be modeled. Passive behavior is distinguished by a lack of eye contact and excessive silence. On the other end of the spectrum, someone who is loud and constantly interrupts and looks at others is said to as aggressive.

Avoid evasions and self-justifications.

Make three crucial points in your message:

Describe your dissatisfaction with the behavior in detail. There should be no charges or pronouncements. There should be no charges or pronouncements.

It is critical to present a rationale for your point of view. Once again, your statement should begin with "I" rather than "you." Before you begin speaking, express your feelings to the other person by utilizing the suitable terminology. This permits the other person to understand and value your actual feelings rather than a generalized perception of your feelings.

Explanation of the implications of their request as a result, you may feel obligated to disappoint others or find yourself unable to meet your own duties. Perhaps they were so preoccupied with the immediate matter at hand that they failed to consider the consequences for others.

Allow someone else to speak in front of you.

Often, all that is required is that you convey your point of view properly to the other person so that they fully understand it. It is conceivable that you will require additional time to achieve progress.

If you continue to speak, you will receive no response, and your assertiveness may be replaced with a long-term complaint. Before doing anything else, give the other person time to think on their actions.

Each time you communicate with others, you may receive a distinct set of responses or reactions. Keep track of all of your experiences so that you may compare them afterwards and figure out what worked best for you. It showcases your knowledge in various areas while also highlighting places where your abilities could be improved. This will increase your confidence.

How to Improve Your Self-Esteem Through Practice

Before dealing with someone's answer, it's usual practice to practice assertiveness. This can be difficult unless you are in a scenario where you are dissatisfied or believe your boundaries have been violated in some way.

Many people find that creating environments where they may practice their speech in a variety of circumstances on a daily basis is really beneficial. Because your statements will be more confident, you will be able to speak more quickly when the time comes.

Consider the following instances in which assertiveness is essential, as well as those in which passive or aggressive behavior is unacceptable. Consider how you would characterize the unfavorable behavior, how it affected you, and how the other person's behavior affected you in each case. To obtain a deeper comprehension of your body's language, replay the discussion in your brain or in front of a mirror.

Chapter 3
Factors that Prevent you from Being Assertive

While we all desire to be assertive 24 hours a day, seven days a week, there are a few roadblocks to overcome. Individuals and situations will do everything they can to undermine your ability to assert yourself assertively at all times. The problem, however, is to design techniques for remaining assertive in the face of these impediments while yet attaining clear results.

Life will always be full of difficulties. This is an inescapable result. In this chapter, we'll look at everything that could be holding us back from being more assertive in light of this situation. a) What are our objectives? We will, on the other hand, not only propose practical detours around those expected obstacles, but will also put you in the right route to avoid them in the first place.

Manipulation of the deciding action has an immediate effect.

Anyone would be perplexed by the individuals they meet and the weird events that occur in their lives. When he heard out that his wife's mother was traveling a Greyhound bus from Columbus, Ohio to visit them in Indianapolis, India, he used to get delighted.

The widowed elderly woman was self-sufficient. Because she didn't appear to be a frequent motorist or traveler, Greyhound was her favored form of transportation. She didn't tell anyone about her plans until she arrived at the Indianapolis city center bus terminal, due to circumstances beyond her control. A person's look (especially if they arrive abruptly from another state) is never a positive sign. That would be deemed exceedingly dumb, not to mention offensive, in the vast majority of cases.

Not only would this have evicted my friend and his wife, but it would have also put her in danger of being threatened. If my friend and his wife had been truly out of town that day, they would have spent the better part of the day detained in downtown Indianapolis. My friend, on the other hand, happened to be at home and available at the moment. When his wife told him to drop everything and rush to the bus terminal during rush hour to pick up an unexpected guest, he was not pleased. He felt dissatisfied with the scenario.

While being carried along by his wife and mothers-in-law, he felt the tugging of his cords. Despite his own troubles, he thought he was acting in the same way as any other husband or son-in-law by allowing his wife's mother-in-law to be rescued. He was unaware that he had been exploited and manipulated in the tense stop-and-go traffic scenario after picking her up and having a brief conversation with her. While we want to be assertive and offer legislation, we are stymied by an erroneous sense of moral obligation. All notions of decisive action have been thrown out the window in such a scenario as a result of others' direct engagement and influence.

To be honest, my friend didn't have many options when he found himself in the situation he did. If given the choice, he would most likely abandon his mother-in-law to the wolves rather than squash the resistance (or at least the homeless hobos of downtown Indy). If he had insisted on keeping his entire schedule, he could have simply rung a cab to take her to the top floor.

To be sure, he was using his usual passive-aggressive strategy in this case. While sending a taxi cannot be used to prove that he left his girlfriend at a bus stop, it can be construed as a message of unhappiness because he declined to personally pick her up. As a result, he's in a classic Catch-22 situation: if he finishes, he'll be stupid, but if he doesn't, he'll be damned.

The real question is how he and others around him got into this situation in the first place. His mother-in-law had organized the entire stressful scene when you arrived, and she was most likely supporting his wife, who was either similarly manipulative or involved in her mother's manipulation. Someone along the way had clearly determined that my good friend was an acceptable target for control and, as a result, liked him.

And why has this individual been dubbed "easily manipulated"? This is most certainly the case, given that he was taught to manipulate from an early age. As a child, his parents may have employed the carrot and stick method to punish him. Such parents are more likely to instill in their children a conditional type of love, in which a parent tells their children, "Oh, I'd adore it if you did that."

Such love is conditional on the recipient's behavior, and a parent's love can be given or withheld dependent on the acts of their children. This just indicates that the child is in emotional turmoil. Consider the following hypothetical scenario: "OK, junior," a mother assures, "you will go to Grandma's place, and you will!"

However, it is possible that the child does not want to meet Grandma and begins to pout for whatever reason. When his child's attention is drawn to him, the dishonest parent asks, "Can you tell me what you're thinking?" "What do you mean exactly? Aren't you in awe of your mother?" "I-I love you, mum," the terrified child says as he raises his head and bumps it.

"Well, if you loved me, you'd smile and go to Grandma's," the mother says as soon as she walks in, playing with her daughter's emotions.

With only a scattering of knowledge about my acquaintance's past, it's likely that he was subjected to emotional manipulation comparable to that which youngster encounter, making him a lifetime target of manipulation. However, I have not got any precise information concerning his life. This is most certainly a long-standing issue that prevents him from functioning as an adult on a consistent basis.

As a result, he is frequently forced to act against his will, and he is fully unaware of these manipulative behaviors until they occur in his presence. If you, too, are a victim of these deceitful cycles, get help from a reliable source to reclaim your freedom. Consider the following hypothetical scenario: Did you grow up in a home where you were made to feel guilty or even undesirable if you didn't meet a certain set of criteria?

If this is the case, you've been socialized to be easily manipulated emotionally. To break free from this pattern, you must first recognize it and make a concerted effort to adjust your future responses to similarly unreasonable requests. Never feel obligated to give up your work because of the whims of others. You must understand that asserting your rights is totally appropriate, and that no one should be able to say that they "do not love you" simply because they disagree with one of your requests.

concern about what others may think

We are all human beings who care about what other people think of us on some level. We may put on a brave face and appear unconcerned, but we all do it at some point. Because if we genuinely cared about what people thought, we'd have no problem burping in the face of a clerk or grinding our teeth in unsightly places during a religious service, all while reclining in one of the churches.

No, if a large enough number of individuals were genuinely careless about what others thought, even a dull trip to the grocery store could turn out to be rather hilarious! Yes, we're all concerned about how other people view us. And, without a question, we portray our best selves when we're in a crowd. Being too concerned with what others think is not the same as being entirely gripped by dread. However, it's easy to picture someone who is very sensitive to other people's opinions being more assertive. You want to be loud and proud, to speak freely, yet even the slightest whiff of mockery sends you fleeing for shelter. So, how can we avoid this situation?

Let us begin by remembering that we, too, have one head, two arms, and two legs, and that everyone else is terrified of us. In other words, humans are included. They have the same problems as you and breathe the same air. As a result, we should fear them just as much as we fear ourselves.

We may believe that others have power over us, yet this is not the truth. Many of your anxieties may be shared by others; they may simply be better at disguising them than you are. Actors immersed in the terror of the stage were originally taught that the audience was just dressed in garments to help them visualize this fact.

This was done so that the performer might picture their audience as a group of individuals lounging in their pajamas on a Saturday morning, rather than a regal (and possibly condescending) woman dressed in beautiful attire and costumes. Despite the absurdity of the situation, the performers did not appear to be frightened by the enormous crowd that had assembled to watch them execute their quick observing exercise. Respect is a concept that cannot be broken. Allowing someone to loom too close to you is not a smart idea. Simply take a big breath and remember that the people you are terrified of are humans just like you, struggling with their own difficulties on a daily basis.

You're afraid of speaking out for yourself.

This obstacle is a little more difficult to overcome than the last one. Because some people are terrified of not only what other people think of them, but also of speaking up and standing alone. As a result, it's possible that someone hasn't adequately established himself in the past and is afraid of expressing their own thoughts and feelings in public.

The strategy is simply modified over time to assist you in gaining more assertiveness. You will not need a significant sum of money to get started. Begin with the most basic details. You could be held accountable, for example, if your neighbor borrowed your power equipment and did not return it after several months. March to the location and demand that the power sources be returned to their rightful owners (politically). If someone criticizes you, merely play your broken record and regurgitate your tools, which you have come to anticipate.

Although this is not a life-or-death emergency, it is a small step in establishing and protecting your basic human rights. After achieving a little objective via such steady effort, you can progress to greater, more difficult obstacles in your personal life, at work, and in other aspects of your life. If you move rapidly, the possibility of establishing yourself will not frighten you.

To avoid offending anyone, you're going with the flow.

People are generally fearful of upsetting the apple cart; therefore, they are hesitant to be assertive. They believe everything is OK and have no urge to produce enormous waves of their own. While someone may look to be content, the truth is that you are definitely wanting to break away and do something great.

It only takes a modest bit of encouragement to persuade such a person to try anything new. Despite having excellent employment opportunities, many people are stuck in a rut. They earn enough money to cover their costs, but they are hesitant to explore new activities. They may even be hesitant to advance in their industry for fear of something disastrous happening.

Someone comes to mind who fits this description well. Greg works in technology and is successful, but he has turned down multiple opportunities to work as a project manager. What is the reasoning for this? He's content with where he is right now. Change anxiety has the potential to stifle our ability to advance.

Greg's clear pleasure in simply getting his mind off things and going about his business appeared to be in his best interests. As a result, he keeps doing the same thing day after day. Whether or not people, like as my buddy Greg, believe they have discovered the key to success, it will quickly become a dull routine.

Boredom will set in quickly in this situation, and you may consider quitting your career. It is vital for someone with this personality type to regularly push themselves beyond of their comfort zone in order to channel their energy into something that makes them happy and satisfied.

Self-esteem is not synonymous with self-assurance. This will suffice for the time being.

Insecurity regarding one's own worth is a typical source of distress for a large number of people. Adolescents and young adults, especially males, have persistent poor self-esteem. Low self-esteem, on the other hand, does not emerge out of nowhere. In actuality, it is frequently the culmination of years of hard work and dedication.

Many children may have been raised by critical parents who taught them "conditional" love, which meant that their love could only be displayed if certain criteria were met. Carl Rogers, a well-known psychologist, argued that "unconditionally positive respect" is the most effective parenting method in the long run. This suggests that love is not dependent on the child's success or failure, nor on the parent's optimistic outlook.

That is not to state that the child is defective, but it does imply that if the child fails, the parent should cease loving them. Unfortunately, many children have been reared by parents who withdrew their love if certain criteria were not reached.

Your father was telling you how angry you were throughout a Little League game, but when you hit the big hits, he showered you with all kinds of attention. Perhaps the effects of the treatment lingered, and you formed an "inner critic," as psychologists refer to it.

When you make a mistake, a small voice deep within you echoes your parents' words to you, telling you how brutally your parents have fooled you. If you want to have a positive sense of self-worth, be assertive, and continue living your life, you must hush the nagging critic within.

While it's wonderful to be thought of as pleasant and welcoming, we can also be "kind" to ourselves when we make mistakes. What exactly am I talking about? What exactly am I talking about? When our ability to satisfy others deteriorates drastically, niceness becomes a serious source of distress. Maybe you've decided that putting your head down and attempting to please yourself will make your life easier in the long term.

While being pleasant and agreeable has advantages, trying to be a truly pleasant person all of the time has disadvantages. Because if your main purpose is to get along with others and avoid conflict, you've entirely lost your sense of assertiveness. Furthermore, when decisive action is necessary, this perfect go-along-to-get-along technique may prove difficult to implement.

Consider a person who goes to the movies with a bunch of pals. Assume that the entire party agrees to go see a Superman movie together. "I understand," you merely murmured, nodding. "That's wonderful; many thanks. Superman is my favorite superhero."

Superman continues to be praised as a result of widespread affection. But then something unexpected happens. Your friends had an epiphany and decided to shoot a Batman film instead of a comedy. They then turn their focus to Mr. Nice Guy, and you express your desire to see Batman as well.

While you may believe you are being kind and charming, your actions have become strange. We look to be dishonest at best and lacking in self-determination at worst since we bounce around like ping-pong balls at the whims of others. Unfortunately, courtesy is only going to get us so far. In order to succeed, we must occasionally avoid consistency, put our foot down, and be a little more assertive.

Chapter 4
Advantages of Being Assertive

There are numerous advantages to utilizing an assertive communication style in everyday situations, which we will cover in this chapter. You should have a clear idea of why assertiveness is so crucial to build and maintain after reading this chapter.

The following are the top assertive characteristics.

1. Increase your self-assurance and self-belief.
2. It promotes effective communication during times of conflict or tension.
3. Increases your classmates' respect
4. A stronger sense of self-worth and self-awareness of one's own abilities.
5. Allows you to follow your own path while being in solidarity with others who do not.
6. Assisting you in developing the skills required to be a better manager.
7. Assist you in developing more effective interpersonal relationships

There are several benefits to assertive communication. This section will go over the advantages of assertive communication.

The individual's body language demonstrates self-assurance in his or her ability.

An assertive communication style is built on self-assurance and confidence. These folks have a confident body language that signals to others their level of comfort in their surroundings. These individuals' body language involves eye contact, which indicates that they are calm but attentive to the discourse. Despite their assertiveness, their speech volume and tone are assertive. They are not scared of physical or symbolic rejection or disagreement, nor are they fearful of being wronged. Assertive people are well-known for their ability to avoid rejection and conflict in every setting.

They communicate in a calm but assertive manner, demonstrating respect for and confidence in their ideas. It's simple to keep a good relationship going when you're in one. Arguing with them while remaining unaffected by their own point of view is the easiest communication to communicate with this type of communicator.

You're content with your existing situation.

They are not looking for obscurity or to exhibit a superiority complex. The ability of this communicator to connect with others without putting on a show is highly respected.

This section will look at some of the disadvantages of three main communication styles: aggressive, passive, and passive aggressive, to help you understand how they may impair your interpersonal connections and relationships.

An aggressive mode of communication

As you've learned in this book, aggressive communication is defined by a righteous attitude, and individuals who employ it do it with zeal that frustrates or disappoints others. As a result, those who engage in this type of communication are frequently disliked by their peers. If you want to get your message across, this method of communication is ineffective since individuals often stop listening when they are overburdened. When looking for understanding and a good listener, you are unlikely to stumble across this mode of communication.

Passive communication is unacceptable.

Disagreement is purposely avoided in this form of communication. If you try to please everyone, you will be disappointed unless you and the person with whom you engage share a common vision.

Individuals who communicate in this communication believe they must tread carefully in order to maintain their feelings, which leads them to believe they are incapable of sharing their thoughts as well. As a result, both parties engage in false dialogues that conceal their genuine sentiments and thoughts. When it comes to issue solving or knowing what other people truly believe about something, this style of communication is ineffective.

What distinguishes passive communication is the manner in which it is carried out.

As previously said, this communication approach is used when a person displays one type of attitude on the outside while sending an opposing attitude through his or her words. When you are afraid and passive, for example, you appear assertive and angered.

This method of communication is ineffective because it causes others to misinterpret whether you are angry or shy, leaving you unable to reply appropriately. Because they are frustrated, they may approach you and communicate their unhappiness with this type of communication. They must try to extrapolate your genuine feelings or intentions from your words in order to determine what you truly mean, no matter what you say.

Chapter 5
Assertive Communication

Friends

There are two types of friendships to consider: those you've known for a long time and those you've only recently become acquainted with. Your new acquaintances are ideal for practicing assertiveness with. You've overcome the initial obstacles and determine that they will play an important role in your life. They do, however, have a limited understanding of who you are. If you want to succeed, you'll have to start from fresh with your new acquaintances. You are absolutely ignorant that you lack assertiveness and have difficulty saying no.

You should now have well defined boundaries, making it very easy to develop a friendship right away. Perhaps you'll see that once you start clearly establishing and delineating what you're comfortable with, others will follow suit. As a result, your friendship may outlast some of your other relationships. There are various actions you can take to help you spot the problem and then seek solutions when it comes to building long-term connections.

    1. Examine how you interact with others.

It's possible that you assume your opinions are insignificant. You may feel excluded from a conversation, or you may be the one who is continuously examining the other person's expression. Whether or not you make plans with another person, the other person will always cancel. Consider moments when you've let your pals down and how you handled the situation. What prompted your emotions?

    2. Keep a journal of your ideas and emotions.

As a result, you'll be aware of all the times when you should speak up. In the connection, you'll notice patterns that need to be disrupted. You not only understand why and when you are wounded, but you also understand how to treat it. Having a newspaper on hand may also assist you in coming up with plausible answers to existing difficulties.

3. Express your feelings to your buddies.

Even if you are up to a certain level, this is not an assertive move in any sense. When you start preparing for a big speech, you will almost surely become anxious. Rather, strike up a polite chat about coffee or a light and delectable beverage. Describe your feelings and your goals for the future.

4. Create techniques to help you and your companion grow your friendship.

Perhaps you and your partner could start a new pastime together, one that you both like rather than one that you both despise.

5. If the negative behavior continues, you will need to increase your assertiveness.

However, now that you've had your first talk, you'll notice that things are a lot clearer. You can tell your friend that you've already discussed it with them and that you've clearly stated your ideas. Be assertive with your pals and communicate your emotions with more passionate language. Instead of the verb "angry," you can use the term "furious."

6. This could mean that your friend is still ignoring you and that it's time to reevaluate your friendship.

It may appear to be more difficult than assertiveness, but if you don't want your point of view to alter once you've firmly established yourself, it's improbable. Remember that those who ignore you are suffering from passive aggressive symptoms, and it is their problem, not yours.

7. Seek out new friendship chances.

You can meet new people while avoiding acquaintances who aren't interested in your company. Enroll in a new sports class or another activity that interests you. You'll almost certainly encounter folks who share your interests.

A good friend would almost always acknowledge your feelings and try to address the problem. You are not required to believe that you are about to lose all of your pals. On the other hand, even the strongest friendships do not always stand the test of time.

Consider whether remaining unsatisfied with this person in your life is preferable to making new friends.

Workplace

Managing interpersonal interactions at work can be as difficult. We all have employees we consider friends and colleagues we avoid at all costs. Certain managers make us nervous, whereas others we'd rather talk to about anything productive. Furthermore, the non-assassin has a much more difficult time establishing his or her place while you are in command.

Despite the fact that we have no direct touch with our staff, we are not passive during our shift. Given the long hours we spend at work, being able to talk freely and without fear of repercussions is critical for us to enjoy our time there.

Employees will frequently go to great lengths to be the dependable and hardworking employee that management is looking for. Without a doubt, our efforts will be rewarded in the shape of the promotion we want.

As a result of your hesitation to say no at work, you end up taking on all of the responsibilities that no one else wants. They will almost certainly ask if your colleague wishes to prepare a presentation. You will be asked to stand in for someone who will be unable to make the call this weekend. If we are unable to decline these new tasks, we will be unable to meet our own responsibilities, resulting in burnout. Aside from that, saying "yes" to work-related requests consumes your social life.

There is no difference between the assertiveness required for personal connections and the assertiveness required for commercial ties. To guarantee that you and others are treated equally, it is assertive to speak with confidence and respect regardless of your rank, whether you are a junior officer or the CEO. While setting individual and team goals is vital, there is no need to push them, and you always have the option of declining. Each of these responsibilities is done while good working relationships are maintained.

To be assertive at work, you must first understand the foundations, which we have covered multiple times throughout this series:

1. Improve your self-esteem and confidence. Recognize your value and what you can contribute.

2. After performing your investigation, decide whether you want to say yes or no.
3. Make brief sentences that efficiently convey your message.
4. Make appropriate use of "I" statements to convey your emotions.
5. Maintain a straight posture and a cheerful expression while controlling your body language.
6. If you're unsure, ask for more time instead of reversing and agreeing under duress.

When making assertive assertions, maintain a firm and confident tone. You have the option of responding without elaborating or supporting your stance.

Rather, under federal and state law, each employee has some workplace rights. Crossing the boundary between law and ethics is tough. You may cross a legal border or disobey a law if you find yourself in a situation where one of your limits must be violated. Men, like women, have made enormous strides in sexual advancement. A hand on your leg or a rope crossing your shoulder may feel sexually harassing to you; others may disagree, but it is still deemed sexual harassment. It is unethical for a member of staff to approach you and request that you make a $20 purchase at the cash register.

- The wording is incorrect.
- Mistreatment of the tongue
- sexual kinship
- Sexual development
- Personal information is available to the general public.
- Confidentiality violation
- Customer gifts have arrived.
- Religious and cultural beliefs are not considered.

If you are employed, you should become familiar with the legal and ethical boundaries that apply to your position. Because not only your personal boundaries, but also legal boundaries, have been violated, this will empower and facilitate your self-assertion.

As part of this strategy, you should double-check your contract to verify that you understand your legal rights and obligations thoroughly. When the law is on your side, it doesn't feel like you're fighting for your own rights.

It's likely that you're not the only one who struggles to make oneself known at work, which provides another perspective for others who continue to struggle. If this pattern of behavior appears to be recurring, know that you are not alone. While it is not your job to solve all of your difficulties, praise for expressing yourself and correcting errors is tremendously useful to your self-esteem and trust.

Family

You are far from alone in making family-related mistakes. It's likely that you've felt passive and as if your life had come to an end at times. It's natural to yell and feel bad after yelling when you're upset. Being assertive in our family has numerous benefits for you, your children, and your grandkids.

Rather than being frustrated and expressing bad emotions, both parties should engage in a good communication. As a result, communication improves. Everyone who participates will gain a better understanding of their own and other people's emotions. Being assertive with your family members will result in more positive communication than exerting yourself, at least at initially.

Don't try to connect the dots between events.

When you compare your children to other family members, you foster a competitive mentality in them, which can harm their self-esteem and confidence. It's all about accepting one's uniqueness and being different is totally OK.

Demonstrate your knowledge.

Mutual respect is required if you want to express your own thoughts. It is vital to try to comprehend and empathize with family members' feelings. Take the time to observe and comprehend each other's feelings. We regularly ask, "Would you like to go out to dinner?" It suggests that you want to go out to dine, but this isn't immediately obvious. "I'd like to go out to supper," you should say instead.

Spreading rumors is not acceptable. When we begin to say too much, we become nervous, and our assertiveness loses its effectiveness. Simply recall and focus on some of the rapid, succinct, and assertive remarks we've made so far. Your body is used to communicating what you are unable to say verbally. While your words may express a single message, your body language exposes your genuine emotions. To protect people's feelings, you offer contradictory messages by uttering white falsehoods, making your message more difficult to comprehend.

The most prevalent type of issue is when our parents do not recognize our abilities to make our own decisions and advocate for ourselves. They may continue to treat us like children, with little confidence in our abilities to direct our own life. This may be distressing since, as an adult, you should be confident in your ability to make sound judgments. Unfortunately, when you consider your judgments or thoughts to be secondary, you are more likely to think and feel about your actions in a secondary manner.

Throughout our educational journey, we have sought to comprehend the emotions of others, particularly when it comes to communication. Regardless of how offended you are by your parents' controlling behavior, you must take a step back and see their point of view. Your parents may seek to exert influence on you in extremely unusual circumstances, which we will examine in further detail shortly. Your parents, on the other hand, are almost undoubtedly scared. You can understand their dread of being wronged or harmed, and it's natural for a parent to want to shield their adult kid from harm. While this may seem silly in your thirties or forties, the older you get, the more they believe they'll need you and want to keep you close.

If you regard your parents as afraid rather than in control, it will be far more difficult to be offended, and connecting with them will be much easier.

Many of my clients and I discovered that providing more than our standard brief, assertive message was more effective than the opposite. You can explain how you arrived at your conclusions and developed your thoughts, demonstrating that you carefully evaluated each step.

Knowing that you've explored all of your options will assist you in recognizing if you've made an impulsive decision.

Manipulation necessitates the application of force. While a manipulative person may be motivated by fear, this is unacceptable given that they have taken advantage of your assertiveness and exploited guilt and shame to attain their goals. Regardless of whose family member you are, you may need to take some time to calm yourself and leave the situation first. Take a step back and look at the big picture – their deceptive methods could be motivated by self-interest and egoism. You may simply want to spend time with oneself, but you're approaching the situation incorrectly. Understanding the underlying cause of your treatment will assist you in evaluating how you will respond.

If the big picture isn't immediately clear, ask for more information about your request. Determine the type of support your father will require if he requests it. Simple job demands may be an indicator of his wish to see you or stay with your mother. You have the option of assisting him if he actually requires it.

If you feel duped, use "I" statements to express your feelings clearly and without attacking the other person. "I don't enjoy it when I'm compelled to do something I don't want to do," I say.

At all costs, interruptions must be avoided. It also prevents you from reaching a decision and interrupts you, both of which are indications that your emotions are untrue. Make a concerted effort not to interrupt, as a tiny pot calls the black scenario kettle. To convey your message, all you need to say is "Please do not interrupt me."

If you have expressed your feelings and the family member has listened and considered everything, you should feel more respected as a result of this conversation. You may need an assertive reminder from time to time, such as "Mom, we discussed how I feel when you insist on my doing something," but it should not contain any assertiveness that makes you feel uneasy or worried about what you're doing.

Unfortunately, despite your efforts, some people will continue to ignore you. Before you can have a joyful, loving relationship with your family, you must first build your own identity.

Recognize and admit your flaws to yourself in an open and honest manner. You do not need to be offended right now because you have not yet done anything illegal. You must, however, recognize that you and your family have limits. You've made those boundaries quite plain to them, yet they've chosen to disregard you. Being assertive with you in the future will make you believe that you have the right to ask for what you want.

If family members continue to press you to do things you don't want to do after you've empowered yourself with assertive assertions ("Graces, but I don't want to," "Graces, but no, I have plans," and so on), you'll need to make stronger declarations or simply say no.

Consider how assertive you were and how you managed to avoid failure. You feel obligated to be extremely assertive since you don't care about this person.

Being extremely assertive is not considered aggressive at the moment. Maintain your cool and persuade them that you'll be able to speak again once they've calmed down and walked away. Take satisfaction in both your great communication skills and your growth.

Partner

Collaboration with a family member or a friend is an option. And you can't simply walk away from your relationship whenever you feel they're uninterested in your thoughts or preferences.

As a result, prior to the attack, we must employ a combination of the techniques described above with our friends and family. To minimize repetition, let's go through the assertive acts that are appropriate in partnerships.

Make a firm foundation for communication.

If you're having a horrible day, don't keep it to yourself because you're concerned about your family. You must be able to speak up when certain feelings occur, rather than waiting for them to reach a boiling point.

Explain to your partner that you don't like it when they leave dirty dishes around the house and that you both need to pitch in on the cleaning.

Please provide them the courtesy they deserve.

Your point is well-considered. The fact that they disregarded the ringing phone implies that they committed a critical error that must be corrected. Keeping your attention on dirty dishes all the time gives the message to the other person that you haven't listened to or valued what they've said.

Allow oneself the freedom to make mistakes.

If you do not pick up your filthy food, they have the right to come to your location and do so. Responding with a click is pointless when someone says, "Well, you left your laundry on the floor."

Don't be a jerk!

As simple as it may appear, we get so used to doing things that we forget to express our gratitude and make requests for items we want after a while. Think about yourself and others in the same way. Despite the fact that we live in the twenty-first century, this is a major source of contention for many couples. Equal treatment should not be restricted to those who work. Compromise and collaborative discussion of issues are required to achieve equality.

Accept no apologies or concessions for your beliefs or goals.

Simply being married or in a relationship does not guarantee that you share the same values and convictions. Instead of making your partner feel awful for expressing themselves, offer comments that reflect your feelings for them. Because "I" assertions are so crucial, they should be presented as sentences beginning with "I feel," rather than "you make me feel."

Distinguish your emotions from your objectives.

Allowing your emotions to cloud your judgment and derail your goals is one thing; allowing them to cloud your judgment and derail your goals is something quite different. Make no attempt to be assertive, even if it is really affirmative, simply for the sake of being assertive.

We may feel assertive in exerting ourselves because of the other person's attitude, but we frequently fear the worst, that he would desert us. When you are assertive in a relationship, one of three outcomes can occur:

1. Your companion will come to appreciate and understand your unique perspectives, limits, and points of view.
2. As a result of the event, a non-abusive disagreement may occur.
3. Your relationship may terminate because your personality types are incompatible, rather than because you have reconciled with yourself.

This may appear to be frightening, and the degrees of 1, 2, and 3 will vary based on the situation. It does not have to be difficult to be assertive in a relationship. It's merely a communication for the sake of conversing. Instead of arguing about differences, accept them and use them to better understand one another.

Children

Allowing children to be self-confident - that is, to comprehend and learn to articulate their feelings and ideas - is a fantastic gift we can give them since it is a practical approach of nurturing confidence. Inadequate emotional education, on the other hand, will almost surely lead to children becoming aggressive or passive, as well as feeling obligated to impose or ignore their own demands and expectations.

If you do not make an attempt to improve your circumstances, it will deteriorate as you age.

So, how can boys and girls enhance their assertiveness?

1. Listening to how they're feeling and paying attention to how they're feeling without passing judgment on their outlook on life.
2. Supporting them in understanding and managing their emotions in such a way that they are no longer scared of them through practice and a more self-sufficient approach
3. By posing useful questions that allow people to completely express themselves.

Consider the following hypothetical scenario: A child is enraged at one of his or her peers. Even if he is encountering it for the first time, it makes no sense to us. He could be sensing how it feels to be angry, afraid, or fearful.

When we act in a way that is inconsistent with what has occurred - for example, when we lie - we are acting inconsistently with what has occurred "Let's be honest: nothing happened. There was no indication of life anywhere. We will not help him cope with the sentiments he perceives or mobilize resources in advance of an upcoming event in any way." Our goal is to bring tranquility back as soon as possible, but our presence will not quiet him down, and his cry will be heard for a long time. Alternatively, our refusal to consider his feelings may make him feel insignificant, leading him to suppress his emotions in the future.

His realization that this struggle, as well as the sentiments he is experiencing, are extremely delicate adult duties is critical to the success of his quest. Only in this manner will the youngster be able to amass the resources required to pursue his or her dreams confidently in the future.

When it comes to young children's emotional development, effective communication is critical, especially when emotions appear to take over. It's difficult to master on one's own because it's a complex skill that requires a variety of attitudes (for example, empathy) that a parent must cultivate in order to produce a happy environment.

Self-assurance and assertiveness are crucial not only for our own and our children's self-esteem, but also for the establishment and maintenance of productive and balanced relationships.

When the situation calls for it, assertiveness is the capacity to stand up for one's rights and articulate one's feelings with consistency and resolve. It is a communication and interpersonal strategy that assists people in developing self-confidence.

It is based on a balance of social abilities, emotions, and rationality, and has no influence on the individual's personality. Individuals that are committed are more inclined to collaborate, resulting in the establishment of equal links.

Assertive behavior results in a joint win.

The purpose of assertive behavior is to overcome differences, discover common ground, and better oneself and one's relationships with others.

The assertive person's goal is to win by collaborating with others. Make no concessions or impediments to the other person's uniqueness.

Nonverbal communication is defined by a firm, warm, and well-modulated vocal tone, as well as an open, direct, and relaxed glance and attitude.

By accepting and valuing one another's points of view, assertive communication promotes egalitarian collaboration and allows us to better understand one another. It is a conversational style that allows a person to express positive thoughts; it is the third communication approach available, following passive and aggressive tactics (both NOT affirmative modalities).

Stranger

So far in this book, we've discussed how to be assertive with friends and family, but what about strangers? What is the golden rule when it comes to strangers on the street? When interacting with strangers, the method is often the same as when dealing with known people: safeguard your rights and maintain a firm stance. When speaking with strangers, several delicate components must be addressed. As a result, here's a quick outline of what you should do if complete strangers confirm your existence.

Take a risk—but not too much!

Confidence is difficult enough to maintain when we can foresee what our friends and family will say but dealing with strangers makes it even more challenging. As a result, while testing your affirmation with strangers, proceed with caution and use your best judgment.

One of my pals (we'll call him Danny) was involved in the following incident a few years ago in a New York City train station. One of my pals, who works for a particular Big Apple newspaper whose name I will not mention, was riding one of the typical New York City subway lines on his way to work downtown.

The man next to him was roughly half the price of the seat to his right, which he could easily scout if he so desired. He was barely able to squeeze into a seat when he realized that the man next to him was nearly half the price of the seat to his right, which he could scout quickly if he so desired. As a result, Danny politely answered, in an attempt to establish himself, "Excuse me, sir, but I believe you've already taken up enough space for your right. Could you please get a little closer to the table?"

Despite the fact that it was a basic request, you might be forgiven for thinking that old Danny insulted the man with every disparaging epithet possible. If the man stood up, he might inquire, "What did you say to me?" "Could you perhaps scoot over a little further?" Danny inquired after witnessing his world-record-breaking technique in action.

Danny, who was getting upset, took a long breath, and gathered himself before responding with a strong "Fine."

Danny was most likely excellent in this circumstance, considering he walked away from it. Danny's blood began to boil the moment he made eye contact with the individual he was chatting with, who was obviously suffering from rage issues. Danny was scared that if he continued his investigation, he would end up in a fight with the man. And what is it supposed to accomplish?

If Danny had won the fight, the cops would have been summoned due to the uproar in the area. Officials, on the other hand, saw only a passing car and Danny's fractured knuckles, regardless of who was behind the attack. Danny would almost certainly have been apprehended and imprisoned for assault and violence at the time. And why is this the case?

An obnoxious passenger will not even move his or her are a few inches onto a seat. What's the deal with this? Danny made the correct judgment when he realized that it was preferable to simply let the situation pass – at least with a stranger. You know, there are times when you have to be really cautious when deciding which fights to join in.

Yes, you are accurate. Yes, you are accurate. We have a horrible habit of judging strangers harsher than we do those we know and love. Those who seek these answers believe that humans have evolved to the point where we can judge random persons we encounter and predict the outcomes of our interactions. To put it another way, we are always evaluating others.

We don't try to be judgmental, but when we're interacting with strangers, we can't help but see red signals. We want to know if someone is pleasant when we meet him. Are they a trustworthy source of information? Isn't it true that they pose a danger? Someone who looks to pose a serious threat to us will be avoided more often.

If you were jogging down a road early in the morning and a gigantic, tattooed muscleman approached you from the opposite direction, you would almost surely give him a sideways glance, whether you were correct or not. On the other hand, if you occurred to pass a small elderly lady, you would be much less worried.

People make hasty decisions like this for the sake of survival. As a result, if you're ever threatened, you'll know exactly what to do. If the tattooed gentleman handled you aggressively, your fight or flight reflex would immediately kick in.

Because prejudice provides us more time to consider these harsh decisions, it permits us to make them more quickly. Being overly critical, on the other hand, can undermine our efforts to be authentically aggressive. Make an effort to comprehend why individuals behave the way they do, even if their actions appear nonsensical to you. Knowing anything about someone's background can boost your confidence in conversations with them.

When analyzing seemingly minor details from strangers, we have a tendency to become emotional and respond in ways we wouldn't expect from recognized individuals. We would not change our minds if a family member accidently crashed into us and apologized half-heartedly. On the other hand, if a random Wal-Mart employee did the same thing, we'd immediately label it a personal attack.

We are inherently skeptical of others and their motives, and as a result, we place far too much emphasis on initial impressions, causing us to get overly emotional. Let's keep our Wal-Mart example going. Consider yourself in a toothpaste aisle, trying to buy your preferred brand when a random lady slips the last tube from beneath your nose. You had to pick up the toothpaste package yourself for a few seconds since her arm flew out in front of you and flung it off the shelf in front of you.

You have the impression that your boundaries have been violated, and you have something to say about it. Even if you don't have the toothpaste she took, you should use your voice to express your outrage at her brazen rudeness. As a result, you clear your throat and exclaim, "I had intended to take that!"

Despite the fact that she knows what you're saying, the lady is being irresponsible by dumping the toothpaste on her cart and grumbling, "Grab what?"

When you step into the warehouse and turn on the lights, you're already at work. "Of course, the toothpaste! I was about to take the previous one when I noticed you had already taken it!"

After that, the toothpaste's teeth yell "You wretched adolescent, you! I guess you'll just have to change brands."

You're weak at the time; you can't remove toothpaste from the woman's cart, can you? Everyone is staring at you now that you're in top condition, and security guards are just a few steps away.

This type of outburst is nearly always ineffective, and those who engage in such public outbursts with complete strangers frequently regret their actions. The current epidemic, which began in the early 2020s, demonstrated that mask use was an issue. Several times, business owners and even customers have attempted to be assertive and encourage certain people to put on a mask in order to be guided through an unexpectedly aggressive storm.

The opposite has also been true, as evidenced by several incidents of masked people hurling insults towards unmasked people. In general, getting worked up over such problems isn't worth it.

Being assertive involves working toward a goal rather than destroying chaos. However, avoid being overly emotional when attempting to resolve a matter with someone. Instead, strive for as much clarity, rationality, and objectivity as possible.

Smokescreen antagonists are most effective when they have dark potential.

As previously stated, we don't want to arouse strangers because we don't know what they'll do or how they'll react. But no one ever said we couldn't completely perplex them! To conceal their actions, they must construct a good smokescreen, as suggested by the doctor.

When someone utilizes a smokescreen, they may avoid a battle or object to criticism. They merely allow you to project a cloud of smoke in the direction of an opponent in order to disguise their movements. In order to garner attention, people will occasionally seek out conflict and attempt to instigate a fight. All you have to do in that situation is fall into the trap of becoming aggressive or arguing with the person.

Even the most violent bully will be unable to talk if you smear dirt in their eyes and make the scene so blurry that they are unaware of what is going on. After all, if they can't see or understand what they're up against, they won't be able to attack you!

The smokescreen approach is based on the audience's passive acceptance. He does not oppose the other person's viewpoint; rather, he agrees with it. Consider the following scenario: Someone yells at you, "You're a terrible jackass!" "OK," you might say, smiling and nodding, "do you think I'm a total jackass?"

It takes people off guard because it's a little out there, and it's ideal for spreading an explosive scenario. "I'm not a jackass; you're the jackass!" instead of "I'm not a jackass; you're the jackass!" "You're the jackass!" you yell. You simply acknowledge the other person's words and go on without replying. If people are seeking for an opportunity to debate, creating a smokescreen eliminates that possibility. After all, it's difficult to argue with someone who appears to be in a good mood.

The actual challenge is expressing your disagreement with the other person's logic while remaining content with the other person. You might, on the other hand, maintain your assertiveness while disregarding the opposite position. Consider the following scenario: In a crowded supermarket, an aggressive woman pushes her heavily laden shopping cart up to the space between you and the next person, as though she intended to push her way to the front.

You will move closer to the gentleman in front of you if you reject to be chauffeured, blocking the woman's attempt to cut you in front of the queue. Despite the absurdity of her actions, the woman groans and becomes agitated: "I'm driving a car with three kids in it! I need to reach out to them!"

After that, you can say, "Oh, okay—you have children in your car."

"And I have to go back!" the woman cries, stressing her plight.

"Yes, you should go back to them," you nodded quietly.

The woman is perplexed because, although appearing to agree with her, you refuse to change your mind word for word. Meanwhile, her cart, which is positioned just outside the check-out lane, looked totally absurd.

She was expecting a fight, but instead she appeared to have discovered a large ear! When someone says this, their words are regarded as having "general truth." You acknowledge their feelings while refusing to agree with any foolish request they may make. Yes, the mother's car has children in the backseat, and she should return to them. This does not, however, guarantee that she will be able to do so without negatively impacting a huge number of paying customers. And we all pick up on certain techniques and strategies. The woman in our hypothetical situation was unquestionably someone who knew how to get what she wanted through drama and emotional manipulation. You may even use a good old-fashioned smokescreen to fool any potential attackers you come across. This, together with the other suggestions, is a wonderful way to be assertive in the face of complete strangers.

Chapter 6
Assertiveness for Women

In today's culture, women are encouraged to assert themselves and recognize their rights, as well as their own interests and goals.

Cinderella's refusal represents feminine empowerment.

Assertive communication is the ability to articulate one's own needs and feelings while also respecting the needs and rights of others within one's shared space of connections; it is the ability to bind true relationships together freely, without feeling driven to satisfy others at any costs.

Regrettably, we live in a world that supports many forms of deception and prefers dishonesty over sincerity.

Women confront the additional challenge of successfully participating in these social games while professing to be unaffected by spiritual demands in the thick of it all.

Cinderella's rejection resulted in incredible transformations: the pumpkin transformed into a carriage, the mice transformed into splendid steeds, and Cinderella's unclean garments transformed into exquisite attire and crystal slippers!

Are we confident this is how events transpired?

Cinderella, what is it about denying that is so tough for you? What are your feelings about yourself? What are your self-perceptions? Furthermore, where can you find the strength to struggle against the imposition and prohibition of infidel women, as well as to reject your fate, at this moment in your dreadful past, which has been marked by loss and exploitation? What makes Cinderella assume that a chance meeting with this intervening element, this Charming Prince, is all that stands between her and a dark and dismal life?

Everyone is talking about it, yet few have heard of it...

To live in total harmony with others and with oneself, one must have a firm grasp on one's own personal worth, a healthy sense of one's own self-esteem, and a firm grasp on one's own human dignity.

Women's validation is crucial in today's world.

The majority of people are uneasy around assertive women because they act in the following ways: they say what they believe, know, don't allow themselves to be hurt, and don't change their minds about their personal worth; they have a clear understanding of your rights and requirements and act in accordance with them; and they are comfortable around other people's rights and requirements. Individuals who can affirm their own identity and principles are effective at finding enough time and space to express their emotions, desires, and deep feelings; those who are afraid are those who are afraid of communicating a "No," which they will almost certainly have to do, are afraid of risking unpopularity, and are afraid of experiencing less or even less pleasantness.

Unfortunately, women have long been encouraged in our culture to see things objectively, to be perfect and sympathetic, to always put others' needs first, and to devote themselves to family, children, and/or profession...

A woman's enormous efforts become equally apparent when she is accustomed to passive things and attempting to imagine the possibilities when she is accustomed to servile and expensive things; in a world where women are compelled to associate themselves with servile and expensive things; in a world where women are accustomed to demanding less and expressing less about their needs, demands, and emotions; in a world where women are accustomed to demanding less and expressing less about their needs, demands, and emotions;

The system expects a woman to make the greatest sacrifices, to cease feeling and being to never consider exercising her rights or expressing preferences, such as not breastfeeding and returning to work as soon as possible. Many people questioned your decision to have a kid, given your ambition to be a successful businesswoman. That, like everyone else, she did it with the assistance of another person, her father, who, despite his right not to be distracted by his personal and professional achievement, does not appear to be an issue.

Women are frequently shielded after becoming moms, particularly in the job. Managers and coworkers are usually quite accommodating to a woman whose requirements have changed substantially due to her new parenthood position. Women are routinely denied the right to select their own colors: they must all be the same! Maintain your spot in the choir; avoid discipline or expulsion; and be adequate or you'll be kicked out. When a woman becomes a mother, she often has only one chance to recognize her new role because she has lost credibility in her previous roles; a child becomes an untrustworthy source of distraction, whereas a mother becomes an untrustworthy element, a lottery machine, and a ticking time bomb to be avoided. Put the needs of the baby (who has already given birth in excruciating pain and at great risk to his or her life) and the family first in this case, dear woman: your life is now theirs; perhaps, when they no longer require your services, you will return to thinking about yourself and your profession.

Certain women make the deliberate and heartfelt decision to devote their entire lives to their families, accompanying and nurturing their children. No, I'm not speaking with another woman. They attempt to strike a reasonable balance between the mother's negating role and other roles and identities as a replacement, feeling that this is the best course of action for their well-being.

The inability of a woman to effectively communicate with her partner, family, or employer prevents her from informing them that her needs have changed, that she has the right to continue caring for her career and relying on her financial independence, and that she requires and is entitled to better support and cooperation from them. Women are more prone to choose a subordinate strategy in these situations rather than taking risks, exposing themselves, expressing themselves, enduring, being content, adjusting, and yielding.

Many women, like Cinderella, learn how to live for the delight of others by never setting boundaries for themselves, others, or society. The mind has lost its capacity for innovation, desire for personal fulfillment, or ambition; the tiny heart, which is far too often filled with passive optimism and the unshakeable belief that everything will be fine; The

Females that are not assertive lack confidence in themselves, their beliefs, and their decisions. They lack confidence and strength; they doubt their ability to change; they do not feel like protagonists of their own lives (which is not the case...); they live a life that someone else has contemplated; and, ultimately, they do not feel like protagonists of their own lives. The weight of those yeses became oppressive, and rage, along with a slew of other extremely potent emotions, erupted furiously after the drama of failing to recognize oneself and feeling the sorrow of an unwanted life had been stifled. When there is no clarity, strange decisions and tough steps are usually taken, as with Cinderella, who feels she has found her only way out, her salvation, in Prince Charming, but has instead entrusted her life to someone else once more.

In reality, rash, impulsive, unheeded behaviors and unexpected outbursts rarely result in "a happy and happy life..." but rather in acrobatic feats doomed to fail, flashes of phony bravery, shaky attempts, and attitudes that lose their dick in a short period of time: a fall into void; and they almost always land poorly, injuring...

The ability to break free from a habit is at the heart of assertiveness, and it can manifest itself in a variety of ways (unfortunately typical of many women). The ability to put oneself in submissive roles in relationships and then say NO when desired; the power to choose oneself without delegation; the ability to be guilt-free if one does not share one's decision. The goal is not to become evil and transform oneself into hens of war, but rather to become combating women who desire and know how to impose themselves on themselves, lovers of life: nothing more, nothing less; and the goal is not to become evil and transform oneself into hens of war, but rather to become combating women who desire and know how to impose themselves on themselves, lovers of life: nothing more, nothing less; and the goal is not to become evil and transform oneself into hens of war

It should make us think about how someone who has worked in a certain way and followed certain patterns for a long time cannot change overnight; they must be willing to practice, participate in criteria, and have the confidence to take appropriate risks. To gain substantial and long-term rewards, you must learn to feel your emotions, put in a lot of effort, and take incremental steps. It also includes the opportunity to make mistakes and learn from them, which is critical at the beginning of a shift that is equally necessary for assertiveness as it is for other abilities.

It could be a good beginning to start addressing your own issues, such as determining what occurs to us when we answer without hesitation. What exactly do we mean when we claim we're in a good mood? What exactly do we mean when we claim we're in a good mood? What are the ideas that are destructive to our health and prohibit us from being assertive? What could be a more powerful thought for motivating us to pursue our goals in a more positive manner? Accept the possibility of becoming less popular and pleasant while remaining kind, progressive, and self-esteeming; accept the possibility of becoming less popular and pleasant while remaining kind, progressive, and self-esteeming; accept the possibility of becoming less popular and pleasant while remaining kind, progressive, and self-esteeming; accept the possibility of becoming less popular and pleasant while remaining kind, progressive, and self-esteeming; accept the possibility of becoming less popular and pleasant while remaining kind, progressive, and self-esteeming; accept the possibility of becoming less popular and

When people choose to conceal their own thoughts, desires, and rights in the face of other people's demands and needs, they pay an unimaginable price: they lose their sense of self.

Chapter 7
Different Communication Styles

The term "affirmation" is becoming more popular in psychology and employee training, and it can be used in a variety of contexts. To gain a better understanding of what constitutes and does not constitute affirmability, it is useful to begin by identifying what does not. To begin with, this is neither a passive nor a violent reaction.

Everyone has left an argument with someone and thought to themselves, "Damn, I should have said that... next time I'll do it differently." We were passive in this situation. We occasionally feel bad about ourselves because we were too aggressive, yelled at someone, or used our expanded right to self-defense: in this case, we reacted furiously toward that person.

Because we've all been in these situations, we can all act passively, aggressively, or assertively depending on the situation. However, in most settings, some persons are more assertive, passive, or aggressive.

Passive

They are people who are constantly on the lookout for other people's needs and are always ready to meet those wants and fulfill those requests in their daily lives. People who participate in passive behavior find it difficult to say no for fear of "conflicts," and as a result, they are readily swayed by others' beliefs and behaviors due to their high level of social anxiety.

These people are respected and admired for their constant availability in social situations, which causes them to assume that this is a characteristic that must be defended in order to keep their standing. However, it is common for someone to "abuse" the passive (spouse, friend, or employer) to the point where he feels forced to say yes even if he does not want to in order to avoid deceiving others and causing conflict and debate. The individual will occasionally try to say no or defend themselves but will thereafter carry out their activities while overcome with sorrow. People who become gradually passive estimate this, whereas those who become aggressively active sense anger, rage, and other repressed sentiments that provide a regular outlet for somatization (headaches, gastro-intestinal problems, stress symptoms).

Aggressive

When compared to passive people, aggressive people appear to be always focused on themselves, and they achieve their aims through coercive and destructive means and conduct. This person works just to gratify and profit from their own selfish desires. He is anxious that if he does not take aggressive action, he will fail to attain his goals, and he believes that any gesture of kindness should be concealed from others as a sign of weakness.

Certain criteria can be met in this manner, but it risks endangering other key areas of one's life, such as friendships, coworker relationships, spouses, parents, and children. Even those who are effective at being aggressive are typically dissatisfied with themselves. He further isolates himself, leading in emotional outbursts of rage, animosity, and anxiety that find a new outlet in the struggle.

Both passive and aggressive actions, it goes without saying, have negative effects for the individuals involved as well as others around them. However, there is a point of stiffness in the midst of the continuum.

When we talk about affirmation, we mean a person's ability to believe in oneself or herself while maintaining healthy relationships with others. Communication is a two-way street, and exceptional communicators respect the rights and wants of others. The assertive person isn't always calm, cheerful, or diplomatic; depending on the situation, he strikes a balance between aggression and passivity.

Passive-Aggressive

Despite the fact that it appears to be an oxymoron, it is a valid state of being. Someone who is passive aggressive is referred to as passive aggressive. If we're being fully honest, we've all engaged in passive aggressive behavior at some point in our lives. If you are angry but want to remain anonymous, you can engage in passive hostility. The majority of people who engage in passive aggressive behavior want to speak up but are terrified of the repercussions.

As a result, the passive aggressor, without realizing it, seeks ways to "pay back" people who have wronged him. Consider the case of an employee who is constantly called in to cover for a consistently late employee and is pleasant to the individual in front of him or her while being filthy behind his or her back. This is a classic case of workplace passive antagonism.

Consider that the target of this passive hostility is blissfully unaware of the intensity of hatred caused by the realization that time is running out. While they may be a little down because of their frequent tardiness, they are not down when called upon to fill the hole left by their passionate, aggressive colleague — in fact, they grin and appear joyful!

What am I referring to? Even while his colleague flees behind his back, the passive aggressor assures the victim of his fury that everything is alright. Consider the following scenario: you arrive late for work and are greeted by a coworker who is cheerful, smiling, and extremely pleasant. Don't you believe everything is in order?

Even if the passive aggressor is unable to address his late coworker, the situation will deteriorate behind closed doors until the backstabbing becomes too explosive for the target to ignore. They will all be in a terrible predicament as a result of the scenario.

While tact — or passive hostility — may appear to be acceptable in some contexts, it has been demonstrated in others to be ineffective. Furthermore, those who have become accustomed to passive aggressive conduct may find it difficult to exert themselves when necessary.

Assertive

Assertive behavior that supports human equality of rights and allows us to act in our own best interests, defend ourselves without fear, openly and honestly express our opinions, and enjoy our rights without risking the rights of others.

To be effective, communication skills must be efficient. It necessitates improving one's capacity to communicate oneself and assert one's viewpoint while also respecting the ideas and rights of others.

If you can't say no, exercising assertiveness will help you deal with a range of situations that bring tension and discomfort in your life more successfully.

While some people appear to be naturally assertive, the great majority of us must learn to be assertive.

Instead of saying "it's horrible" or "you can't cook," use the assertive communication method of saying "I don't like that" to convey your unhappiness with anything. It is not certain that improving your assertive communication skills will result in you achieving what you desire as a result of your efforts. This advancement will also boost your interpersonal interactions.

It is not sufficient to just convey your point of view to people who may or may not agree with you. Trying to persuade people is fruitless. This is something you must exhibit for yourself in order to demonstrate that you can behave appropriately and with self-control.

Confidence is founded on a strong sense of self-worth, and communication facilitates the development of self-esteem.

Chapter 8
People-pleasing Mindset

When you consider their situation, it looks that they are fighting a never-ending struggle. We've come to meet our people's most fundamental wants, and we've spent some time getting to know ourselves and figuring out what makes us happy. The method should not be considered as a quick cure because acquiring the ability to say no in an appropriate manner takes time and trust.

During the early phases of my life, I discovered that making little changes to five very minor things that I did was really useful. Because these five products were self-contained, I saw benefits practically immediately. Several clients have remarked that implementing these five measures assisted them in gaining momentum, which motivated them to continue doing a good job as the advantages accrued. Examine each of these five stages in greater detail.

Step 1: Become aware of any sick people in your near vicinity.

Pleasing others gets so ingrained in our minds that it is impossible to separate it from other aspects of our personality over time. It's like folks who don't aware they're always cursing. Many individuals despise foul language, but because of their bad habits, others find it simpler to deal with them.

Pleasing others does not indicate that they like you, especially when individuals in your immediate area benefit from your personality. Even if you subconsciously realize what you're doing is wrong, you won't place a high priority on maintaining a pleasant mood in public because you're striving to improve, simplify, and enrich your life.

As a result, it is up to you to seek out opportunities to demonstrate compassion to others. We've already expressed our satisfaction with the person's primary characteristics; now we'll look at how we decide whether or not to say yes to something we don't want.

If someone suggests you're having a split-second emotion, inquire as to what you're feeling. Nervousness, depression, fear, fear, panic, and rage are all emotions that can be felt. We can't just disregard feelings and point a finger at them to see what they are.

When you ask yourself what you want, you will not receive a straightforward yes or no response. Some aspects may sound amazing, but you should approach the problem differently.

Consider what you require - the usual instinct is to satisfy others; however, if you look beyond this, you may find that you require an hour at the gym or a long bath in the bathroom.

If you're unsure, consider what you're terrified of. A large portion of our inclination to say yes is motivated by fear of the repercussions and how others would react. Perhaps you're concerned that if you say "yes," you'll have to go through the process again in the future.

You are not a bad person because you have the audacity to say no. It should not be one's goal to become a self-centered, unhelpful individual. We're attempting to strike a balance.

While you may not be able to say no right immediately, being aware of a setting that others find appealing may assist you in deciding what to do next. By asking yourself the four questions listed above, you can better determine whether or not you want to accomplish something and why.

Step 2: Develop a grateful attitude.

Two things normally happen when someone who is pleasant to be around receives a compliment. The shock catches us off guard, and our defense mechanisms, such as denial, kick in. When it comes to expressing our gratitude, we are literally at a loss for words.

We make an intentional effort to validate compliments as frequently as feasible. I've heard classic examples of people fawning over someone's clothes while also claiming that they are lousy at fashion and that their sister chose or gave them the outfit. When someone compliments your supper, you answer by talking about how much fun the evening was or how simple the dish was.

These conditions may not appear to be very harmful at first look but take the following scenario: your wife or spouse compliments you on how wonderfully you decorated them, and then you attack them because you believe they are funding your efforts. You may not only have wounded their feelings, but you may have also created a dispute between you and the other person. Furthermore, people will be hesitant to say great things about you in the future. As a result, I was hesitant to say, "thank you," believing it would encourage me to continue talking. Instead, I learnt to respond to compliments with a range of different words:

- Whatever you've done or said has been greatly appreciated by me.
- It means a lot to me.
- What's new in your life? You have a favor to do for me.

When someone says, "I like your hairstyle," I can now answer, "I adore that," and the conversation is effectively done. I would have already loaned the money to my girlfriend. Positive attention should be welcomed rather than avoided, and this exercise is an excellent example of how to do so.

Step 3: Demonstrate Your Love for Yourself.

Unhappiness with one's life sometimes reflects dissatisfaction with one's own self-esteem and a struggle to love oneself. This is frequently due to a desire to prioritize others or a lack of self-confidence, which prompts us to focus on our defects and disliked characteristics.

Some of the positive actions mentioned above can be implemented into your self-love routine, and you will notice a difference in your everyday life as a consequence of your efforts to care for yourself. You may discover that your relationship improves over time as your sense of self-worth grows if you can build self-love. We'll begin with some of the most fundamental methods for making someone fall in love with you.

1. Always keep a newspaper nearby.

Newspapers are a fantastic medium for airing one's grievances and feelings. It also allows you to study them and then focus on the positive aspects of your experience as a result of them. I cannot emphasize enough how important it is for you to keep a journal because it allows you to be absolutely honest about your feelings without worrying about what others think. A notebook is a fantastic tool for continuing your journey of self-discovery.

    2.   Make a list of all you've accomplished thus far.

This is yet another strategy that will only help you focus on the positive. A list of your achievements is an excellent approach to remind yourself of your ability. Then, whether with others or by yourself, celebrate your accomplishments. Be fully honest in this section, and don't add anything to the list just because it was someone else's idea or because someone helped you.

- Completing a project successfully
- Begin a new course and complete it successfully.
- When a book comes to a close, it's time to put it all together.
- to perform at one's best in a sport
- achieving the weight-loss goal you've set for yourself

    3.   Schedule time for physical and mental recuperation.

As admirers, we have a tendency to spend our life based on the assumptions and beliefs of others. Only when we fall short of this ideal of perfection do we become too critical of ourselves.

It is also necessary to physically retreat from daily stresses and duties. This is also a challenge for us because we spend a lot of time volunteering and assisting others. As a result, I recommend beginning with five minutes every day and gradually increasing to thirty minutes as you build confidence. You can meditate, exercise, read, or listen to music as long as you enjoy the activity.

    4.   Enjoy your alone time.

I was terrified of being alone, but it provided me with the opportunity to reflect on things I may have done differently or better in the past. I'm craving after it right now. To fully love oneself, one must first learn to enjoy oneself in the company of others. Being alone does not imply depression or loneliness. It enables you to continue discovering new things you enjoy or detest, as well as participating in activities you might avoid if you were in a crowd.

5. Forgive yourself for previous faults.

We all stroll down memory lane and dwell on our follies since we have all made mistakes at some point in our life. Examining your mistakes in judgment will help you develop a better understanding of yourself. To gain someone's devotion, though, you must first forgive yourself for your sins and move on.

6. Travel is required.

This is the most challenging but also the most rewarding experience, and once you've done it, you'll surely want to do it again. While traveling alone, it is possible to get to know oneself on a deeper level by visiting new places and cultures. Because you are not distracted by the feelings and ideas of others, being alone allows you to be more honest with yourself.

It is critical that you begin to appreciate yourself right away. You only need your own intelligence and determination. Others' opinions are no longer a source of stress, and there is no need to be frightened of offending them. There will be no one around to witness you taking these precautions.

This made great sense to me because I knew I'd be making little changes straight away. I didn't have to worry about the implications because no one in my circle of friends or family was aware of my activity, and I was able to learn more about myself. The majority of self-love advice is ingrained in your personality and the way you live your life. Others may occur less regularly, but I'm still keeping a diary to record my victories fifteen years later. I travel at least once a year, whether for a weekend trip or a week-long vacation in another country. When people ask if they can follow me, I smile and politely answer, "No, not right now."

Step 4: Organize and prioritize your requirements.

We live in a world where your own desires appear cruel or arrogant in relation to the desires of others. It's practically impossible to please everyone, and while the theory is straightforward, putting it into action presents extra challenges. Consider why it is necessary for you to understand how to prioritize your responsibilities in the first place.

If one does not prioritize one's own needs over those of others, it is simple to burn out and have nothing left to give. It makes me think of how, when assisting passengers on a flight, you should always put on your oxygen mask first. Similarly, while some may want to wash their hands with it, you have earned the right to satisfy and be content with your own needs. When I first started researching into this, I was astounded by how many people suggested "Learn to Say No" as a solution.

Yes, without a doubt; you're one of my particular favorites. Accept yourself just as you are. Remind yourself that you are welcome, even if just occasionally. Look for opportunities to save time. On a daily basis, we all form tiny habits, such as playing a phone game or using social media. If you can get rid of these items, you will feel liberated for a while.

Make a task list - Be careful not to add chores that have been given to you by others to your list. Use the time you've saved to finish your responsibilities; you may be tempted to call a friend or do a favor for a friend, but resist. You've made some time for yourself, and you should use it wisely.

Establish an everyday pattern - While we all want to break out of our routines now and then, keeping to a routine will increase your chances of satisfying your needs because they will be ingrained in your habit from the start.

Change your mindset – While it may be more challenging, you are not required to say no to everyone. Take a few long breaths to relieve your humiliation and replace it with the understanding that you have the right to prioritize your own needs.

Spend one day per month - Once you start scheduling time for yourself on a daily basis, seeing a whole day in your calendar becomes easier. This day should be a mix of tasks and personal pursuits, or you should begin with a half-day.

Step 5: Create a mantra

A mantra is a short statement or group of lines that you repeat to yourself over and over to urge yourself to do something. They have evolved emotionally and physically, but our goal is to use them to change some of our negative habits and behaviors.

A mantra is a powerful tool for changing one's mental state, and the benefits are immediate. On an emotional and psychological level, pleasing people is motivated by a desire to be liked and accepted by others. Our personal aspirations and life experiences are permanently imprinted on our thoughts. A mantra's purpose is to release you from guilt and the notion that you are not as deserving of yourself as you believe.

Here are a few mantras that can permeate a person's mind:

- You have a lot of potential.
- My criteria are very important to me.
- I have the right to be content.
- I am a powerful force that cannot be stopped.
- I'm ecstatic.
- My dreams have a tremendous lot of meaning for me.
- I anticipate that you will hold me in great regard.

It's worth noting that none of these short lines contain any negative language or make any predictions about the future. They are intended to act as a reminder of the changes you want to make right now, both consciously and subconsciously.

Mantras and phrases can help you start your day off right with a positive, firm perspective, or they can help you settle down and have a good night's sleep, or they can help you do both before going to bed. When people began to reciprocate my sentiments, such as when I wanted to say no but was still given the option, I found that my chant was beneficial.

It doesn't take much work, and the benefits are almost instant. Because some of these will be more tough than others, I purposefully placed them in a more difficult order to make them more difficult. You'll probably definitely learn that taking a vacation by yourself isn't a viable choice right now. You may feel compelled to inform people and explain your reasoning. You may not want to explain how you overcame your parents or why you left if it does not make you feel at ease with them, especially if they are concerned about you and are attempting to talk you out of it.

All of the tactics presented thus far are helpful in maintaining and increasing your ability to say no. Following your initial exposure to these strategies, you'll discover that you're more capable of setting boundaries in your relationships and other elements of your life. The next step is to have a deeper understanding of the situation and determine how to set boundaries. We're also on the approach of defeating one of the most difficult anxieties to overcome: rejection.

Chapter 9
Build your Confidence

It's reasonable that the terms "trust" and "self-esteem" are often used interchangeably. These two characteristics are associated with the tenacity required to achieve our goals, objectives, and ambitions. The fact that one follows does not exclude the other from doing so as well. While you may be confident in your abilities at work, you may be lacking in other areas of your life. It is aware of your objectives and your abilities to achieve them. That decision is made for you. We all have self-esteem, which is described as how we perceive ourselves and others, as well as how we interact with the outside world. Self-assured people are more prone to believe in their talents.

In this chapter, we'll discuss how to boost your self-esteem and improve your capacity to trust others. Not only do you learn assertiveness skills and how to say "no," but you also get the courage to speak up for yourself.

It is common to have a tendency to be hard on oneself. We may experience social anxiety as a result of weight-related comparisons to others, particularly celebrities. As a result, a number of daily activities, from eating a delicious meal to having sex, become difficult.

Other people's perceptions of us, not just physically, but also as individuals, may make us uncomfortable. You may be concerned if you believe your actions do not conform to a cultural norm. Perhaps you do not consider yourself to be a member of any particular social group.

Our concerns about the appearance of our bodies and our food troubles are inextricably linked. You may also experience uneasiness or despondency. While improving one's self-perception may appear challenging, it is possible to do so in little increments. Over time, even the most insignificant ingredient can have a tremendous impact. Consider the following scenarios. Now.

1. Be aware of your surroundings.

There is a small voice within you that is always giving erroneous information to your mind. It's past time to harness this voice and develop a new one that balances out the negative aspects of the existing situation. Every morning, remind yourself of something fantastic to look forward to. It should also not be overly large.

For example, I'm fairly glossy, I love my calf muscles, and I know a lot about this and that. Create something new the next day. Keep a notebook next to your bed and begin writing a list of everything.

2. Accept that no one is perfect.

This is simply not possible. Mary Poppins, on the other hand, appeared to be immaculate in every way. Perfection should never be your goal; instead, aim for continuous improvement.

3. Everyone's existence contains defects.

We do not put off purchasing anything or sending a crucial email because we are lazy. We don't wake up thinking, "Gosh, I hope I make a lot of mistakes today." Errors occur all the time! Errors occur all the time! People with poor self-esteem are more likely to make the same mistakes. Unfortunately, our emphasis on what went wrong causes us to lose sight of the task at hand, increasing our chances of making errors. The best course of action is to accept responsibility for your error, apologize, and go on with your life.

4. Set aside some time for oneself.

Not so that you can catch up on work or clean out your inbox, but so that you can do something you enjoy. Regardless of your gender, take a wonderful bubble bath while listening to calming music and burning candles. Allow yourself to enjoy yourself.

5. Quit comparing yourself to others.

While her stomach is flatter and her six-pack is firmer, these improvements do not characterize her or imply a higher quality of life. You or a family member could be in an abusive relationship or have a medical issue.

6. When it comes to the portrayal of the body,

Our distinctiveness is part of what makes us so appealing. For a few minutes, listen to Baz Luhrmann's song "Everyone's Free (To Wear Sunscreen)." Several of his suggestions are quite helpful.

"Appreciate your body and make the most of it. Don't be concerned about what others think of your job. It is without a doubt the most potent weapon you will ever possess."

7. Improve your self-esteem.

If you approach the stages of self-esteem development with a more optimistic mindset, you will see an increase in your self-confidence.

There are numerous characteristics that show your true capability because our own doubts stem from thoughts of inferiority.

- Before you begin, comb your hair, shower, shave, and put on your clothes.

I'm not trying to minimize your intelligence but following these simple standards will help you feel more at ease in the morning. "And I know," my girlfriend replied when I asked why she felt the need to shave her legs before putting on jeans in the hope that no one would notice. Whether you're meeting with current or new business partners, it's critical to prepare as much as possible ahead of time. Prepare for your trip by practicing what you'll say, anticipating inquiries, and investigating potential study locations.

- Positive activity

We've previously worked on developing our thinking skills; now it's time to use them in other aspects of our lives. Positively respond to the bad characteristics of other people's personalities and look for the positive aspects of every scenario. Along with evaluating your own optimism, be certain that your point of view is backed by the presence of those who share it.

- Make an educated business judgment.

We need to be around by people who share our view on life, who are joyful and self-assured. As you immerse yourself in the atmosphere of a can-do attitude, your energy will soar through the air.

- Keep your distance from people who tell you that you are incapable of accomplishing

Establish goals and divide them into smaller, more achievable bits. That's because we didn't handle things properly in the first place. By breaking down a large objective into smaller ones, you can generate momentum and strengthen it as each one is successfully fulfilled.

- Make an effort to learn a new skill or knowledge every day.

We've heard it before, and it's being said again for a reason. Education for self-empowerment is a wonderful way. Physically, everyday study is not essential; nonetheless, continuous learning should occur at all times. Maintain a reasonable grip on the circumstance, whether it's your job, kitchen, or entire home. After things have cooled down, you envision having more control over your life.

- Kill one's own flesh and blood.

Every day, we have chores we wish to finish but are afraid we won't be able to due to a number of factors. Going the additional mile may be necessary when traveling in a new location or going on a date, to mention a few examples. Make careful you don't make the same mistake I did by attempting to climb Mount Everest. You will succeed if you approach a problem from a tiny angle. If you want to pay someone a day visit, you should first create an online dating profile before approaching the first person you see. Each modest accomplishment increases your self-esteem and confidence.

- Recognize and develop your own strengths.

Those who lack trust frequently devote an unusual amount of time to areas where they are deficient and need to improve. Consider your accomplishments throughout your life to increase your trustworthiness. What traits aided you in accomplishing this

- Appreciate your limitations

Whatever your limitations are, remember that you can work around them by setting goals and breaking them down into smaller action plans.

- Assess your linguistic abilities

By inhaling deeply and staring them down, you can increase your sense of security. Never underestimate the power of a smile. Because a smile makes the other person happy, they will almost certainly reciprocate, making you feel even better.

- Pay close attention to your personal requirements.

Nutrition, sleep, and exercise are important not only for your physical and mental health, but also for giving you the energy you need to deal with life's obstacles and other people.

To be able to say no, you must first be self-assured.

Consider your self-esteem and confidence to be a faucet in a bucket. Each drop will be unique, and your bucket will quickly fill up. The more methods used, the faster the water flows and the greater the benefits.

Chapter 10
Setting Boundaries

Boundaries are similar to the unseen bubbles that encircle us. They are always present and with you, but you only notice them when you look at them. Both safety and happiness have limits. You can put pressure on yourself to become more aware of your limitations, but don't push yourself too far. It demonstrates that if you have solid boundaries, you are incapable of allowing others to cross them.

Boundaries are set up to ensure your and others' safety. You will be safeguarded from overwork if you follow their advice. They indicate when you or another person should come to a complete halt before becoming annoyed. When someone breaches that line, it sends a message to everyone else that there will be consequences.

When you create limits, you acquire the ability to be yourself and be honest. Individuals will not be able to accept their limitations until they recognize the distinction between themselves and their restraints. Consider how you would react if someone invaded your personal space. While this may be a physical obstacle for you, you're more interested in getting closer to it or seeing how far you can get before collapsing. These people believe they have the right to communicate their sentiments and opinions, no matter how they may affect you.

This is because they allow you to acquire the trust of folks in your immediate surroundings. Those who despise constraints, on the other hand, can simply disregard them when they are most needed. They are terrified of upsetting someone and causing a rift in a connection. Individuals who enjoy crossing boundaries may do it because they are terrified of being told no or offending someone else. It doesn't matter how much it restricts or hurts them as long as they can alleviate the misery of someone else.

Setting boundaries is an excellent method to strike a balance between compassion, self-care, and self-control. You are self-assured enough to set boundaries that others should not breach in your presence. When one is troubled or suffering, self-kindness entails giving oneself comfort and confidence.

Healthy borders improve mental and emotional well-being, influence the behavior of others, aid in the prevention of tiredness, strengthen personal autonomy and independence, and aid in the development of identification. Setting adequate limits is essential for self-care.

By establishing clear limitations, you can reduce stress and increase fulfillment in your professional life. When we embrace compassion for others, we may experience compassion for ourselves. When we see people in distress, we build empathy for them. When we recognize our own grief, we must express compassion for one another.

It's critical to practice setting boundaries with our inner critic. Consider whether a second individual was there in your situation. If you are not promoted for something you could have done better at work, for example, your inner critic begins to blame you. If you have compassion for someone and recognize that dispute is an unavoidable part of life, you may forgive them for their faults. If you commit a mistake, you can show yourself compassion and forgiveness. Prepare your response to a friend in a similar scenario.

We can keep our grief bottled up if we ignore our bad events. When we choose to ignore our emotions, they might accumulate to the point of erupting. Instead of ignoring them, welcome them like guests in your home. Allow yourself some time to get to know them, your comfort, and your therapy, and be patient during this process. Make no attempt to overcome your emotions faster than is absolutely required. Allow them to have some alone time. As a result of your activities today, the risk of experiencing these emotions again has increased.

Accepting that everyone makes errors and that we all live with an open heart toward reality demonstrates compassion for oneself and others. The ability to deal with criticism and flaws is referred to as self-compassion. Everyone makes mistakes, whether they are conscious of it or not. Instead of being so harsh on yourself, consider it an essential part of life that everyone must go through.

Even when we want to, we are frequently unable to create boundaries. We may be able to impose limits in some places, but not all, depending on the circumstances. Certain conditions make setting limits extremely difficult. Our capacity to overcome these constraints will determine whether or not our efforts succeed.

Boundaries of Various Types

We have the potential to set limits in all aspects of our lives. Limits can be set for your sexuality, personal space, property, thoughts and emotions, energy and time, ethical and cultural ideas and behaviors, and religious beliefs and practices. Ethics, psychology, emotion, verbality, and physicality each have their own set of boundaries that can be crossed in a variety of ways. Our preconceived conceptions of what is right and wrong are challenged by ethical boundaries. Psychological and emotional limits have an impact on who you are and how you see yourself. To break down psychological and emotional barriers, judgment, dishonesty, criticism, and humiliating language and behaviors can all be employed. In some cases, gas lighting might act as a breach. Individuals can violate these lines by exploiting information about you that you voluntarily shared with them.

If you cross these lines, others will make fun of you, your thoughts, and your feelings. You crave public humiliation, embarrassment, and torment. These individuals make a concerted effort to garner sympathy from others while also holding them accountable for their own choices and situations.

Verbal boundary violations are intended to restrict you from speaking or discussing yourself in public. There is a possibility that you will be interrupted. Verbal infringements include slander and character assassination. It's reasonable to believe that infringing on bodily boundaries implies someone else putting their hands on your shoulders without your permission. This category includes invading your personal space and even claiming possession of your belongings without your permission. Physical infringements include privacy violations and faults, but they are not the only ones.

Employees must be transformed into objects of pleasure for their superiors on occasion. They feel compelled to speak and act in certain ways in order to keep their employment or be considered for future advancements. Regardless of their personal convictions, the employer expects these employees to make sacrifices for the company. Supervisors frequently believe that their thoughts and opinions are more valuable than those of their employees or subordinates. Managers may find it easier to persuade their staff to do things they would not otherwise do since they have greater influence than their employees. Setting limits can help you protect yourself from this.

Setting boundaries has a multitude of benefits, including increased self-esteem, independence, and the conservation of emotional energy. When you impose limitations on yourself, you are prioritizing your own well-being. You've established a clear boundary between yourself and the rest of the world. Long-term relationship troubles can arise if you are hesitant to periodically bend certain limits. If you're hesitant to disclose more about yourself with someone, you can't expect them to fall in love with you and remain forever.

If, on the other hand, you continue to stray from the boundary, you may want to reconsider your strategy. Women are more likely than males to impose gentle limits because they feel responsible to satisfy others. You can save emotional energy by setting boundaries. Because you failed to create limits, allowing others to walk all over you will make you despise them. Setting limits can assist you avoid feeling enraged by other people's actions.

Individuals' boundaries may alter based on their location, level of comfort, and other circumstances. We can set different constraints in different scenarios thanks to our adaptability. This allows us to pause and reflect on our own perspectives, as well as what might happen if a border is crossed. As a result of this emotional space, we are susceptible and changeable. We may observe the world and define our own boundaries after engaging with it. If we do so, we can make the shift between emotions smoother.

It's a matter of personal preference, and everyone's preferences differ. Boundaries are defined by elements such as culture, heritage, religion, societal tendencies, family relationships, and life experience. We come from a diverse set of families and backgrounds. Each of us has our own set of challenges to overcome, as well as our unique methods for doing so. As we develop and evolve, we may choose to shift our boundaries. As we obtain new experiences and information, our perspectives may evolve to reflect these new developments. While we are all unique, we must all have faith in our abilities to navigate continuously shifting borders.

It is vital to be informed of your legal rights and obligations when deciding on your boundaries. You have the right, for example, to see your own needs as equally vital as those of others. Accepting failures and mistakes is something you have the right to do. Because it is difficult to remember that we have these rights, we may believe that we must be harsher on ourselves.

When you recognize and believe in your own rights, it is much easier to defend them. You will no longer console and soothe those who violate your rights in this manner. This keeps us from becoming emotionally drained. If you believe that anyone can push you over your limits, pay attention to your intestines. When you experience grief or rage, you've almost likely passed a dangerous boundary.

Your body will demonstrate that you are capable of dealing with the issue (heart rate, sweat, tight throat, stomach, chest, etc.). You may clench your teeth if someone close to you or a member of your family warns you that you are dying. Keep an eye on how other people handle your borders. Do you recall when we discussed the top three values? Consider how you felt when your personal boundaries were questioned. Someone may have threatened a member of your family or your entire family, which is most likely one of your most essential values. When specific constraints are pushed, you will experience similar emotions to how you feel when a different constraint is pushed.

Establishing And Sustaining Boundaries

It is up to you to determine the boundaries. You decide whether or not to hold the event, how many people will attend, and where it will take place. Boundaries are a great way to organize and govern your life. Setting boundaries should be suited to your unique tastes and life goals. When you set boundaries and commit to your health, you acquire self-respect.

If you wish to make any new ones, look over the ones you already have. Keep account of how you came up with them and the limits you faced. This enables you to examine your life and discover areas where new boundaries are needed.

You could establish boundaries if you recently witnessed something that you don't want to see happen again, or if you want to prevent something from happening in the future. Limits can be set in a variety of ways.

1. Be assertive and believe in yourself. Assert confidently that what others say or do will have no bearing on what you say. They will motivate us to push our limits more frequently if we can do so even once.
2. Improve your understanding of when and how to say "no" in acceptable situations.
3. Ensure a safe working environment. When investigating one's feelings, avoid both hurry and self-criticism. You do not need to yell at yourself when attempting to solve a problem.
4. Put together a support system. You need individuals in your life who can put their trust in you and rely on you to say "no" when you need to.
5. Consider it and see what you can glean from it. Keep note of the initial contacts that occur after activating the barrier. If you're satisfied with the outcome, don't touch the border again until you're ready to change it.

Consider a time in your recent past when you were hurt or upset. Have you ever made yourself feel uneasy by using a curse word? When we are upset, we may impose this constraint on ourselves.

Some of us are now unable to maintain the restriction because of the great emotional pain we are experiencing regardless of the conditions. When you set emotional boundaries, they may be inaccurate or overly strict. If you choose to cross that boundary, you might blame yourself or others for the results. While setting quick boundaries in stressful situations is natural, it is vital to reexamine these boundaries once you have regained your calm.

If something makes you uncomfortable, you are not required to regard the sentiments of others while establishing boundaries. Many women are terrified of the implications of reporting sexual harassment at work. Despite her belief that her boundaries have been broken, she believes she is unable to reestablish them without jeopardizing her work and coworkers.

To set limits, it is necessary to be conscious of one's feelings. You must learn to differentiate what makes you happy from what makes you unhappy. Pay attention to your sensations to determine when you need to set up a barrier.

You will feel safer if you keep your surroundings protected. It helps you feel safer to know that something is less likely to be damaged or destroyed. There are both physical and mental "locations" for you. You are capable of defending key assets while also protecting oneself.

To safeguard your region, you must first recognize the value of privacy. Is there anything you'd rather not disclose right now that you're going through or thinking about? It enables you to store energy and use it later. Some of us have an inherent need to be safeguarded since our health and quality of life may suffer as a result.

- You can secure your locations in a variety of methods, including those indicated below:
- Your things will be protected in a lockable drawer or safe box.
- Instead of a traditional diary, keep a password-protected digital journal.
- It is not a good idea to send e-mails or messages to your personal e-mail address or phone number.
- PINs, codes, and passwords should be used on devices.
- Utilize the device's Do Not Disturb and Silent modes.
- To prevent hurrying at the last minute, plan ahead of time.
- When you are not at your workstation, send an "out of office" response.
- Remove any notifications and programs that you aren't utilizing while working from your phone.

Taking time off improves physical and mental health, as well as work performance, quality of life, and a range of other challenges, according to a recent study. If you are always in communication with your employer, you may feel obligated to be present when it is necessary. This could lead to issues in a person's personal life and relationships.

Seeking assistance is one of the most efficient ways to boost your motivation and self-confidence.

- Families
- Partner
- Friendships
- Workmates
- Mentors
- Therapists

You can support your physical and emotional boundaries. If you're experiencing difficulty creating or maintaining a boundary, seek guidance and assistance from members of your support team.

Your support team will assist you in remembering why the boundary was set up in the first place. You can confidently and unconstrainedly navigate the scenario using your previous experiences and examples. Even in the most terrible of situations, they have the potential to persuade you to cross your border.

Chapter 11
Active Listening

Effective listening is required for conversational skill. Active listening includes paying attention to our interlocutor, using proper language, and asking questions and making remarks that show our real interest in what he or she is saying.

Human experience is inextricably linked to empathy and active listening. To do so, you must first understand your own point of view and be conscious of how you communicate - both verbally and nonverbally - in order to capture not only clear messages, but also implicit signals that are more directly tied to your thoughts and aims.

As a result, we'll be less motivated to continue discussing the account, to offer early guidance, to create our own ideas, to evaluate what they say, or to encourage our partner before they've had enough.

Posing questions to oneself such as "What are you trying to say to me?" "How do you feel?" may also aid in active listening. If we continue to speak in this manner, the other person will likely believe that we are skilled communicators and that conversing with us is enjoyable.

Active listening and reformulation are frequently used in tandem. It entails paraphrasing our interlocutor's message in our own words and then asking him to clarify whether we accurately articulated what he was trying to communicate or if we misread or omitted something important.

It facilitates understanding another person's message, correcting any flaws in our view, and communicating our communication. "We don't go to the movies very frequently," a woman may say to her husband when she is bored, wants to see a movie, or simply does not want to be at home. If they believe this is the case, they may question, "Do you mean you want us to go today?"

As a result, by responding to the wife, you can assess whether she correctly interpreted her initial message or whether she want to say anything else. In any event, if you don't understand a response, ask the person to repeat it and confirm that you understand what they said.

It's possible that the reformulation reflects the interlocutor's feelings. If the lady in the preceding scenario exhibits exceptionally irritated nonverbal communication, her husband may remark, "You appear to be ill."

Active listening and reformulation facilitate communication for the following reasons:

Because he acknowledges our predisposition for misrepresentation and is willing to correct it, rather than believing his first assessment is correct and responding accordingly, the recipient of the communication receives and understands it as accurately as possible. If the sender's interlocutor's rephrasing does not correspond to what he initially intended to say, the sender corrects it.

It conveys to the other person that they have been recognized and welcomed, which enhances their self-esteem.

It contributes to the continuation of the conversation by assisting the participant in broadening their perspective, feeling more at ease, and speaking more honestly and fully while paying attention to and empathizing with what the other person is saying.

Our joy and strength are increased for the benefit of the other, resulting in more successful interpersonal connections.

It may also be advantageous to encourage our interlocutor to listen carefully and repeat his or her remarks. One way is illustrated in our example (given the tendency we have to tune in). On occasion, we can contact him personally (for example, when we believe it is crucial that another person understands what we said) and ask something like, "I would be really grateful if you could tell me what you understood about what I said." It's also incredibly successful when the message is critical to you, or your interlocutor and the communication is extremely emotional. When it comes to compliments, it's a two-way street. It is possible to both offer and accept them.

Please extend your deepest congratulations.

"Loyalty" refers to the act of displaying a positive attitude or sentiment for another individual. They frequently express appreciation for the fact that the other possesses a characteristic or feature that we respect. All of these are appropriate allusions to your behavior (such as "you're a terrific buddy"), your appearance (such as "that haircut looks fantastic on you"), or something you possess (for example, "I very much enjoy your house").

Praise is vital in interpersonal interactions because it promotes self-esteem, which is a basic human need, by emphasizing the positive features of the other person.

In order to gain this critical reason, the person who has become more appealing must deliver genuine compliments, and others must be willing to gratify him. The significance of complimenting and expressing thanks is well recognized for a variety of reasons. Among them are the following: We all value genuine compliments on our appearance. Someone who is valued on a regular basis is less likely to feel rejected by the other when the relationship is difficult or contested.

If we have previously displayed a sense of joy and genuine and regular love for the other, we are less likely to have confrontations or misunderstandings when we are compelled to express a negative emotion or defend our legal rights in front of another person, as this creates a nice climate. You have the right to express positive feelings for the other person whether or not they share your sentiments or points of view.

- Garner's lobbying activities are more effective when the following conditions are met:
- Check to see if the individual with whom we're speaking enjoys them.
- Make an attempt to persuade them of your sincerity (it is not enough that they are).
- Compliments from coworkers and other affirming behaviors that demonstrate attention and respect are valued.

It is preferable to share your personal thoughts and sentiments, such as "I enjoy...", "I am glad...", and so on, rather than generic assertions such as "You are fantastic."

Describe what you admire about each other and why. Instead of saying, "You're incredibly fantastic," say, "I appreciate you listening to me and encouraging me."

Praise persons we know will forward our praises to the appropriate person. A third party may make a positive remark about another individual. It's critical to avoid appearing dishonest and seductive; for example, if we ask for a favor, we shouldn't do it.

If the other person finds them difficult to accept, include a question to help them accept them. If you do not wish to react to compliments in this fashion, you will not be forced to do so. Someone might respond, "I admire your coat; was your ordinary coat chopped off?" He can disregard the accolades and focus on who is the most skilled at cutting them.

Chapter 12
Saying No is your Right

What comes to mind when you consider declining an offer? You may believe they have been tricked or angry, or that they are attempting to make you feel bad in order to influence your decision. You could be accused of being aggressive, uncooperative, selfish, or "not a team player," among other things. In this chapter, I'm going to push you to come up with a new way to say no. We'll discuss why saying no can be tough, how to say no more successfully, and most importantly, why learning how to say no is sometimes vital if you want to live the life you desire.

If saying no is difficult for you, it may be helpful to begin with some of the reasons why you can't say yes. On numerous instances, I've witnessed people prioritize the needs of others over their own. This is not always practicable, such as when newborns and little children require assistance with their fundamental needs. However, there is no reason to continually prioritize others' well-being over one's own, and while making decisions, it is vital to evaluate how one's actions effect one's own well-being. This is a well-known story that can be read in a number of ways depending on your point of view. Assume you're getting ready to board an airplane for the sake of argument. After securing your seats, you began sorting your possessions. The plane is almost ready to be retracted from the door, and the necessary passenger safety briefing has begun. When the flight attendants reach the section where they detail the protocol to be followed, keep an open mind if oxygen masks are deployed. They're making an essential point.

It makes no difference whether the tone is funny or serious, as it is on Southwest flights and most other airlines; each time we hear it, it conveys a clear message: you must put on your mask before assisting someone sitting nearby. It's normal to believe that in a life-threatening scenario, there's a strong desire to aid others before donning one's own mask and breathing apparatus, similar to that of a tiny child. It's natural to feel selfish at first when you're afraid that your youngster isn't receiving enough fresh air. Consider the repercussions if you are unable to put on your mask until you have recovered from your own lack of oxygen. If you do, neither you nor the child will benefit from your actions. While creating a feeling of balance in one's life may not always involve the same level of danger or dread as an in-flight emergency, the concept that you are less capable of caring for the wants and wishes of others in your life if you do not take decent care of yourself remains true. When your personal life appears to be in order and your basic requirements are addressed, family, friends, and coworkers are far more likely to show up for you.

When life becomes challenging, it is natural for relationships to become strained. For example, even if you're attempting to help people, resentment can wreak havoc on relationships. You will be able to preserve a sense of serenity and tranquility if you take care of yourself and avoid things that do not seem appropriate for whatever reason.

Some folks have difficulty working with me because they are unsure of their own self-worth. If they respond negatively, it demonstrates that they are unable to reconcile their own desires with the needs of others. It's not always easy, but remember that you're a one-of-a-kind person who, like everyone else on the earth, deserves to be happy.

If you judge your worth by how you compare yourself to others, it's time to reconsider. Seriously. I'm not going to blame everything on social media; after all, people have always compared themselves to superstars, models, and rock stars, as well as their friends and families, long before this medium existed. When the figures are considered, however, multiple studies show that social media is ultimately hazardous to our mental health. Another study published in The Lancet Child and Adolescent Health Review discovered that accessing social media "quite regularly" is associated with increased psychological distress, particularly among young women. It reminds me more of a story than a documentary. People use social media for a variety of reasons, like reconnecting with an old high school acquaintance or promoting a well-known event. I mainly published articles about how I burned my scratched eggs to distract myself from my scratched eggs, or how I spent 20 frustrated minutes looking for my car keys (which were always in my pocket), or how I realized that my apparel online looked better on the website than it did on me. I'd rather show you a photo of my delicious lunch, my new hairstyle, or how much I liked last night's performance than write about it.

Never believe that another person's life is better than yours or that they "deserve more" in some way than you because practically everyone attempts to market themselves positively. Social media may be a tremendous tool if you understand and respect the medium's positive and negative aspects for what they are. Maintaining contact with friends who have moved away, conversing with people you may not have met in person (interact with other Facebook readers at TheMagicOfNoGroup.com), and learning about entertaining, interesting, or troubling events in your town or around the world are all made possible by social networking sites like Facebook. Simply make certain that it does not become a mirror in which you are judged. As previously said, you are a one-of-a-kind individual with an unusual combination of skills, interests, and abilities. They start with this story, rather than informing you how it has a more interesting life, better-behaved children, or a more "important" biography.

Another prevalent misunderstanding is that if we say no, people will abandon us; however, as the story demonstrates, this is not the case. If someone like this came to your door and persuaded you to volunteer for a charity, help a friend with their next move, accept an invitation to a family member's child's band concert, or agree to an evening out with your spouse this weekend, you should be cautious. Although this is not always the case, your capacity to say no should indicate the depth of your relationship. While it's natural to want others to be happy, what matters is if you're unhappy with yourself for refusing to buy new windows from the person who just knocked on your door. If you find it difficult to say no to an unfavorable request, the information on the following pages may help you change your mind.

While others may disagree, the vast majority of people will know that no response is reasonable and will not be surprised if they hear it from time to time. A link's lack of balance could suggest a serious problem, which is described in greater detail in Chapter 10, No, Your Friends (and Family). In contrast, the individual who approaches you at random and tries to sell you anything does not hear you very often throughout the day. Even if you disagree with your reaction, you will hear it again later that day. They have no reason to despise you until they are familiar with your identity and past, even if they disagree with your response. Furthermore, if someone knows and likes you, there's no need for you to change your viewpoint simply because you declined a request. Nothing appears to be a huge issue, but it is a typical occurrence in daily life, and everyone is used to hearing it.

Take into consideration the following: Instead of feeling bad about saying no or fearing that someone may dislike you, consider the following: To begin with, saying yes isn't always the best decision. If you tried to live this manner for even a day or a week, you might understand why it doesn't work. Due to your failure to deliver on everything, you will be unable to aid individuals who have requested your assistance, and you will be fatigued from attempting to keep everything going effectively. While no one likes to be insulted, I believe it is reasonable to assume that hearing "no" is less bothersome than later realizing that someone is unable to finish an assignment. Taking it a step further, your persistent sense of excess is most likely not bringing you joy. As a result, by saying no to some requests, you can minimize stress and improve your performance as a friend, colleague, employee, or parent to people in your life who rely on you. Finally, you must find a balance between your own desires and the desires of others around you. One thing you and I, as well as the rest of the world, have in common is that we all deserve to be happy. One method to accomplish this is to prioritize your personal well-being as well as the well-being of those in your near area. While this may appear to be a pleasant circumstance, it is absolutely fine to take care of yourself and ensure that you have what you desire.

Six strategies to help you feel more at peace with the word "no":

Remember the worth of your time. Others will not value your time if you do not value your own. If someone at work (other than your boss) asks you to do something, act as if you are the boss and examine whether you would want anyone to spend time with your team to achieve the task at hand.

When you are asked to accomplish something, examine whether you believe your time is being well spent.

If you're asked to do something you don't want to do, try to imagine how you'd feel if you had to. Increase the excitement of your experience. Consider your reaction as a result of that. (Hint: avoid anything that makes you feel worried.) You're probably certainly not feeling any better while completing the task.)

Put yourself in the shoes of the person who just requested something from you, and then demand the same thing from that same person. Consider whether you believe that is a reasonable request. If this is the case, you should not be embarrassed to decline the offer.

If your children request something, offer it to them right away while considering whether you would give it to a friend's child who requested the same thing. From this vantage point, if the request looks to be ridiculous, it is most likely yours as well.

Furthermore, if a customer request something that appears to be out of the ordinary, determine whether other consumers are willing to pay for it through your company. If that's the case, you've discovered a potential sales opportunity.

Allow me to add one more piece of advice: as I already indicated, it is vital to research how your beliefs can be implemented. One method for putting it into action is to practice or practice and practice. They don't just play; they spend endless hours polishing their skills and strategizing what they'll say and do onstage. No, you do not need the services of a coach; but, if this makes you nervous, you should practice. This is especially true, in my opinion, if you want to say no but don't know how. The first step is to decide if you want to deny the request outright or use alternative tactics such as lowering the request, delaying it for a longer length of time, or assigning work to others. Close your eyes and visualize the dispute in your mind's eye once you've determined what to do. Simply consider your current location, what is going on around you, whether it is day or night, and so on. Increase the richness and realism of your experience to the greatest extent feasible. Then, to start the dialogue, visualize the ideal outcome or exceeding your expectations. Take a few deep breaths and enjoy how lovely it feels after a pleasant conclusion to the conversation. Then, with your eyes open, act as though you're chatting. Repeat the approach if you continue to feel uncomfortable or afraid, or if you are tempted to avoid confronting the situation. Repeat the therapy two, three, or five times more if necessary. Because this is a fast workout, you may repeat it as many times as you wish until you're satisfied with the outcome. It's also important to be open to the chance that the outcome will differ from what you imagined, but that everything will work out in the end. You may discover that the discourse in real life differs from what you anticipated, and that you do not always get the intended results, but you can remove your nervous expectation from the mental image and approach the subject with calm and faith. If the interaction does not go as planned, you will be less prone to being exploited. If you're shy about speaking in front of a group, try this strategy and see how your relationships alter as a result.

You'll notice that as you become used to it, it doesn't get any easier, but rather becomes a crucial part of the discernment process. I'm not proposing that you always say no. Indeed, I believe that anyone who reacts to a reflection with a yes or no will produce unnecessary problems. The "yes" person will have too much on their plate as a result of being overburdened with unfinished tasks, will be resentful of their duties, and will struggle to be joyful. The person who is always saying no will almost likely have difficulties. They may be viewed as disobedient or difficult to control at work. They may have strained relationships or connections because they do not adhere to cultural norms of giving and receiving or compromising, as well as because their interactions with others are strained. If you want to prevent conflicts, you must strike a balance between setting boundaries and cultivating healthy interactions with your surroundings. It may appear to be a delicate balancing act at times, but the advantages often outweigh the effort.

Chapter 13
The Power of Positive Language

Positive language is an extremely effective approach for improving interpersonal interactions. Expressing regret for one's conduct is one of the first things that inspires individuals to be pleasant. When you say, "I'm sorry," you acknowledge that you made a mistake. You recognize the poor situation and express regret for the outcome. As a result, some people say things like, "This isn't your fault," while others say, "I'm sorry." These expressions allude to someone who has been damaged or troubled.

Instead of saying, "I'm so sorry I'm late," you may say, "I appreciate your patience while I came." Thank you is an excellent approach to convey your appreciation to someone else. If you have done something wrong or failed, instead of expressing "I'm sorry," address the matter constructively. Rather than saying, "I'm sorry, but I'm unable," say, "I wish I could, but I have other responsibilities."

Positive language can help people build solid ties. If you speak positively about other people on a regular basis, you can maintain the energy balance between you and them. By continually apologizing, you lose authority to the other person.

Positive comments can have a significant influence on how others perceive you. Imagine yourself as more joyful, lovable, kind, and approachable. People are ready to assist you because you are constantly offering polite and helpful remarks. As a result of your efforts to help people feel better, you may amass a big and devoted following.

Positive language conveys a desire to converse by displaying a readiness to engage and participate. People are more inclined to engage in conversation with you and feel more at ease around you when you interact in this manner. Additionally, the likelihood of being allocated to a cohesive and conscientious group increases.

Consider the following hypothetical scenario: You're in a check-out line, and the cash register isn't operating properly, so you're going to have to wait a long time. When you approached the checkout, she stated, "Everything has been sorted; we appreciate your patience." "I'm sorry that didn't work; it wasn't my fault" is worse than "I'm sorry it didn't work; it wasn't my fault."

Many people who come into contact with you will leave in a better mood than when they first met you because you say thank you instead of, I'm sorry. Others in your immediate surroundings, such as employees, may be able to incorporate your idea into their everyday life, resulting in a more positive tone of voice. Simply by employing pleasant language, you can have an indirect effect on a big number of people.

In writing, positive statements can be utilized instead of several negative ones. After some practice, you'll find yourself repeating this sentence.

- "I'm sorry, but I can't help you with your request because you didn't supply me with all of the necessary information."
- Rather than telling someone what they haven't done, find out what they require. There's no need to justify your lack of self-care to others when you can just ask for what you require.
- Instead of "I'm not sure," say "I'm not sure."
- Instead of "I'll see if I can find someone who knows more," use "I'll see if I can find someone who knows more."
- If you wish to assist others, avoid using the phrase "I'm not sure." o The phrase "I'm not sure" is meaningless. If you truly want to assist them, you can point them in the direction of a resource where they can obtain the information they require.
- The phrase "How significant is this?" should be avoided.
- Practice responding to the inquiry, "How essential is this?" "How does that relate to our work?" you could ask.

Negative terminology is being phased out in favor of positive terminology. Consider remarks that are fundamentally harsh or disagreeable as an example. Consider a novel approach to reaching an agreement or making a request for something more favorable.

Instead of emphasizing on what you can't do, use positive language to highlight what you can. It implies that you are invested in the conversation and trying to attain a favorable ending.

It is possible to present unpleasant news in a positive light, so easing the burden on others. It may be simpler to relay unpleasant news if it is presented in a positive perspective. If you're at a loss for words, especially in the thick of a bad news cycle, consider the following.

- Bring the positive parts of the situation to the forefront.
- Show a willingness to assist.
- Make a point of emphasizing how you can assist.
- Make statements that do not elicit defensive responses from others.
- Empathy should only be displayed when absolutely necessary.

After all, expressing empathy means that you are unsure of how you will act. When delivering terrible news, however, it is critical to demonstrate empathy in order to avoid making the recipient feel attacked or alone. You are entitled to use affirming words at work, with your family, and in public.

Conflict is possible.

Disagreement, as silly as it may appear, has the capacity to open up a whole new world of possibilities. When confronted with difficulty, there is the possibility of both gain and loss. You have the capacity to arrange and regulate your activities, which increases your chances of success. You can get a sense of how the other person reacts in certain situations. You assess your feelings and sensations. You will examine how each party reacts to a situation in which one of them raises his or her voice during a dispute.

Confrontation can help you develop a better knowledge of your ability to resolve disputes. These abilities influence your options and the courses you take to complete the battle.

If you can solve difficulties more successfully, you'll have a stronger bond. If you are certain that you can engage with another person without getting into a fight, you will feel more at ease in any setting. This communication approach produces strong, productive, and healthy partnerships. Visualizing a solution to the problem might give you a brain exercise.

You can learn new skills during battle. Was there been a time when you were in danger before learning something you didn't know? Or were you fully oblivious that you had made a mistake? These are the times when you discover fresh information that you can apply to future issues.

Throughout a combat, you can practice your decision-making abilities. Every battle group will require your assistance in determining which course of action to adopt. You will feel relieved and in command of the situation after the conflict is finished.

Conflict can occasionally produce poor effects. Allowing specific people to leave or intervening in situations that cause pain, discomfort, or stress are two choices. This could be advantageous. Certain relationships may deteriorate with time, regardless of the degree or breadth of the partners' shared history. While you are immersed in a disagreement, you may have the opportunity to purge your life of harmful people and energy.

When you're in the midst of a fight, you have the opportunity to demonstrate your emotional intelligence. You may have seen that the other person becomes overly emotional, and it is time to move on.

It is also feasible to view a situation from a different angle. You may agree on a subject but be unable to communicate your agreement due to differing points of view. When you believe you've mastered all facets of a subject, it's easy to maintain your modesty.

Chapter 14
Speaking your Truth, Communicating your Needs

Our ability to express ourselves determines our ability to contribute and progress. When we are entirely honest with ourselves, we increase our chances of developing better, more honest interactions. It's time to discuss the principles from Chapter 2. What were your own revelations? Were your responses unexpected? Did you know which of the top three would be yours before you started?

If we don't have a clear understanding of our passions, we may become frustratedly sidetracked from our regular activities. Consider a time when you were proud of something you built or restored, or when you finished a task. While you're standing there appreciating your success, keep an eye out for your inner smile.

Do you remember experiencing a surge of energy near the end? You acknowledged your self-satisfaction and claimed that you will continue to do the things that make you happy. The event's allure vanishes all of a sudden. You don't appear to be a part of the process, and you appear to be going through the motions. You've lost the zeal for life that you once possessed. You're well aware that being creative entails a lot of nos. When you consider something that others haven't considered yet, it can be terrifying and baffling for them. The bulk of people are opposed to creative efforts because they are uncomfortable.

They are not pleased with the lights or the developments. People who love it frequently assume that by expressing themselves, they are depriving others of space and attention. Others, on the other hand, wish to share their ideas and thoughts. If you can find creative outlets for your expression, you can boost your self-esteem. You express yourself when you engage in things that you enjoy. Some folks will be unable to complete this task. We'll offer some advice on how to improve your communication skills.

Activities

The most intriguing aspect of stimuli for the mind is that they force you to think about them. You come up with new and old ideas, and you are quite delighted with something.

The following habits can assist you in expressing yourself:

- creating a drawing
- Photograph
- Writing is a kind of communication.
- Jig or waltz?
- Putting together a diagram
- Constructing.

You have a good time and the power to make your dreams come true. Instead, you focus on what is in front of you. When you're in the zone, you'll know if you're communicating effectively. You can work quickly and efficiently while finishing a big number of chores. If you become interested in the action unfolding in front of you, you may lose sight of your surroundings.

Social

You have the ability to express oneself socially, as well as the inverse. You are expressing yourself when you speak about your passion. Your pupils may dilate, your voice may become more assertive, and you may have a stronger desire to walk. However, if you are shy, putting yourself out there and avoiding speaking alone may be more challenging.

Being pleasant is usually misconstrued as timidity. It's the same as providing one-word answers because you're afraid to say anything else. Shyness is also associated with being a people person since it motivates you to say what you need to say in order to avoid awkward conversations.

When people around you freely express themselves, you may feel envious or even resentful that they are able to act on their wishes while you are unable to. Some people may even assume that they are immune to sadness, embarrassment, or seclusion. Keep the following list in mind as you work on increasing your ability to talk effectively in social situations.

The act of embarrassing oneself is referred to as self-embarrassment. You must present yourself as the most gregarious person you know. Inquire about their preferred alcoholic beverage. Is this a coworker of yours? Inquire about their weekend plans.

Consider taking a course to learn more. Cooking, painting, and sculpting are a few examples. It's foolish to try to think of a topic to discuss in this way. You are free to share details about your activity.

Maintain an optimistic attitude. Overexerting yourself in preparation for social meetings might lead to exhaustion on the day of the event. It is more advantageous to keep a positive mindset in order to accomplish more.

At all costs, avoid self-pity. Have you made a grammatical error or gotten your words off on the wrong foot? Everything is operational! It's something that almost everyone does. It's something that almost everyone does. Exit the building after taking a big breath. You can prevent being eliminated from the game by conversing with yourself. A slam dunk to end the third quarter.

Make a cheerful expression. Smile. A grin not only enhances your beauty but also your entire health. Furthermore, you pay more attention to other people.

Practice is the key to mastery. Practice. Choose a neutral topic and mentally sketch down ideas for future conversations. You might wish to discuss it with a friend before presenting it to others.

After making a positive social connection, move on to the next one. You have a lot of energy after leaving a pleasant social gathering.

Use a story to your advantage. Have you ever had a particularly humorous experience that you'd want to share? This anecdote can be used to break the ice in a variety of circumstances. You take a breath to speak and deliver a part of dialogue that is pertinent to your story.

The capacity to express oneself can be extremely advantageous to one's health. When we express ourselves, our brain reacts differently? Regularly participating in creative self-expression and maintaining healthy brain chemistry can help prevent depression, dementia, and a range of other diseases.

Speaking is an effective means of expressing one's thoughts and feelings. Conversations have the ability to alter the course of people's life. A chat with another person can have an impact on us, whether it's a two-hour self-help session or a casual interaction while waiting in line.

Conversation recipients are typically more influenced by a conversation than the speaking participants. However, just because they are not affected as frequently as the speaker does not mean that the speaker is not influenced by his or her own words.

Your prefrontal cortex will be activated if you listen to someone else without placing judgment on them. The executive brain is housed in the prefrontal lobe of the brain. The prefrontal cortex is essential for personality expression, decision-making, and complex cognitive task planning. We are in charge of the primary managerial functions listed below (hence calling it the executive brain).

The following are executive characteristics:

- The ability to detect and distinguish differences between competing points of view.
- Enhance your knowledge of the most significant and least important distinctions.
- The distinctions between being lovely and being evil are becoming increasingly blurred.
- "Rationalization" refers to the process of justifying a decision.
- A hypothetical idea
- Administration
- Emotional control is a vital talent.
- Reality's interpretation
- Make educated guesses regarding the outcome.

The ability to stop from engaging in socially inappropriate actions.

As you can see, the prefrontal cortex is home to nearly all of the thoughts and behaviors essential for the formation and maintenance of positive relationships. This is due to the fact that our sense of self is critical to the prefrontal cortex. If we are aware of our own identities, we can create more honest encounters.

The left brain is related with positive aims, feelings, and approaches. The right side of the brain is preoccupied with negative emotions and avoidance. Furthermore, dopamine and receptor sites associated with motivation and reward are more active on the left side.

Those who are harmful to their own delight can enhance prefrontal left-brain activity. Positive emotional experiences are associated with increased right prefrontal brain activation.

Patients suffering from depression may have an overactive right prefrontal cortex on the left side of the brain. Depressed people may find it more difficult to connect exceptional goal-oriented behavior and thought if they have fewer left (positive) access channels. Because the left side is associated with rewards and motivation, higher positive activity leads to increased punishing conduct.

When we speak, we trigger a reaction in our frontal brain, signaling to others that we are inventive and goal oriented. Improved cognitive reasoning and creative thinking have been linked to increased prefrontal cortical activation.

When we participate in an enjoyable activity, neurotransmitters such as serotonin, dopamine, and oxytocin are released, especially when we do it with others. That isn't to say we won't do what we want or take the time necessary to find ourselves. This contributes to our happiness. As a result, our brains are in charge of how they are dispersed.

We may freely express ourselves if we do not allow others to influence our words and actions, and if we do not allow others to affect us. This may cause an adrenaline rush, giving us a burst of high energy. We may be able to take a deep breath of fresh air after the mask is removed and feel liberated.

These compounds not only make us joyful, but they also have a number of health advantages.

Serotonin:
- It improves mood regulation and alleviates anxiety and despair.
- The possibility of assisting in the healing of an injury.
- It aids in bone health maintenance.
- With correct bowel movement management, it improves.
- Possesses the ability to govern and influence sleep.

Dopamine:
- Assists in mood regulation
- It helps with memory and attention.
- Has an impact on movement
- How do depression and anxiety affect our lives?
- Is predisposed to psychosis.

Oxytocin:
- It raises the chances of being identified.
- It boosts people's self-esteem.
- Today's culture's emphasis on sexual and reproductive health
- Contributes to the expansion of each other's links.
- It promotes the formation of interpersonal bonds.

When we want to express ourselves, we have the option of being cheerful. These drugs can benefit you in a variety of ways, including enhancing your ability to communicate.

Isn't it true that making a positive social commitment or engaging in a pleasurable social interaction offers us a boost of energy? Our point of view has shifted, and everything appears to have been reset. Because of the energy we are experiencing, we are responsible for these substances.

Different means of communication

The ability to express oneself in a healthy manner allows one to live a more real and satisfying life. You can be your authentic self while also enhancing your self-esteem. Speak up because it's simpler to emotionalize, believe in yourself, and create the life you want when you're free to do so.

You have several options for expressing yourself.

1. Self-expression occurs when you are able to describe your own feelings clearly and expressively. This provides you with greater hands-on experience dealing with a wide range of emotions.
2. Develop the ability to notice and accept your feelings. Recognizing and paying attention to our feelings can be difficult. Many people may find it challenging to express their emotions to others. In this case, emotions are typically humiliated or embarrassed. Being conscious of your emotions, on the other hand, may assist you in channeling your energy into something constructive rather than feeling afraid or confused.
3. Incorporate celebratory aspects into the ambience of a special event. Decorating is a terrific way to express yourself creatively. Sections, colors, patterns, shapes, and sizes, among other things, can be created. Having all of these traits helps you to think with many sections of your brain at once. You might try harder to express yourself through your environment.
4. Painting as an art form. Painting is an excellent way to obtain a better knowledge of your emotions. Think on the color palette you want to utilize in your property. Isn't this a beautiful color scheme? Perhaps you're happy or enthusiastic. Is the color purple blue? Depending on your mood, you can be happy or sad.
5. If you learn something new, you will be able to accomplish something you have never done before. This assists in acclimating your mind, body, and thinking style to the unknown terrain. This enables you to take advantage of the

situation's novelty and express yourself through your new activity or interest.

Put together and perform a dance routine. Dance. Your emotions have the power to create anxious energy. Emotions can have an impact on both your mind and your body. When you're happy, your muscles are relaxed and ready to move! They may stiffen or shake if you are in a poor mood. When you dance, regardless of the style, you allow your body to move. You can move to the beat of the music as quickly or slowly as you choose, as long as you let it flow. Your body language and gestures can be used to express your thoughts and feelings.

6. Make travel arrangements for a vacation. You can discover new relics and visit their sites all around the world. You are more sophisticated and well-rounded than the ordinary individual in this sense.
7. Make a new friend. Make a new connection. You might strike up a chat with them to strengthen your friendship.
8. Modify your appearance. Clothing is one of the most potent ways to express oneself. Colors, materials, patterns, and other design aspects can all be combined. As a final resort, consider adopting a pet. Purchase a pet. Believe it or not, you can trust your pets in the same manner you would trust another person. It allows you to express yourself through your thoughts rather of just thinking about them.

Chapter 15
Verbal and Non-Verbal Language

N on-verbal Language

Respect is heavily influenced by a person's perception of value. As a result, you must focus on communicating your identity effectively through your body language. Body language, when used correctly, can aid in the relaxation of others in close proximity to you while you are present. Consider these guidelines to help you be more aggressive in your interactions if you haven't previously.

As needed, adjust the angle of your body.

They must persuade others to visit them. If you don't know how to perform anything properly, you'll lose a lot of respect from others. You can affect how people view you by adjusting the angle of your body. When you withdraw from other people, you emanate an air of insecurity.

It is vital that you face them when attempting to project confidence and thus pique others' attention in what you have to say. It is preferable if you like them; nevertheless, this is not always possible; so, use grace in your contacts with them to ensure a nice and courteous meeting.

Make use of your facial expressions strategically.

Face expressions are an important nonverbal mode of communication since they may transmit a great deal of information. You may be seen as afraid if you have a blank expression on your face in front of a huge group of people. If you do not smile, the audience will read your absence as an indicator that you do not enjoy being in their presence. Even while a wider grin is prudent, it is insufficient.

Your continual smile may benefit a small percentage of people who do not want to be on your side at first. You must learn to be yourself and let your face expressions merge naturally. There is a problem in that many people are completely unaware of the message they are sending. If you ask a question and do not receive a response, you may wonder what went wrong. Following that, practice producing comfy and dumb facial expressions. Once you've mastered your facial expressions, you're ready to move on. Consider your reactions and document them as if they were part of a real-life experiment.

Raise your shoulders slightly.

The way you look at your shoulders reflects your mindset. Your sinking shoulders indicate that you are on the second level. However, if your shoulders are drawn up, it shows that you are not afraid. Maintaining appropriate shoulder posture is simply sending signals to yourself that will aid in the development of confidence. When you are self-assured, you send forth signals that people want to follow.

Consciousness of the Observer's Eye

When you're talking, the other person likes to fix their gaze on your eyes at odd intervals. Your eyes can express your emotions and reflect whether or not you're paying attention to what's going on around you. Think about how other people perceive you. You will almost likely be rewarded with the same level of respect if you demonstrate compassion for others.

When it comes to eye contact, it's critical to stare the person you're talking to in the eyes for a few seconds at a time in order to build trust. Be wary if you make direct eye contact with them, as they may interpret this as open hostility. Avoid blinking frequently, as this may cause people to become distracted, and determine if you have a tick or if something is wrong with you. Looking at your watch or touching the corners of your eyes is inappropriate since it suggests latent mistrust about what is happening right now.

Sitting

Your posture is just as crucial when you're sitting as it is when you're standing. During a conversation, your seating position may disclose your level of focus. Establishing your authority and demonstrating that you genuinely believe what others say about you demands caution.

The best course of action is to sit up straight and reach out with your hands to touch the back of the chair. Slouching conveys an impression of laziness, which diminishes your image and the respect you have earned from others. Avoid causing a commotion by resting your hands on the arms, kneeling in it, or folding it. Lean in closer to appear more engrossed in the conversation and to emphasize your points more clearly. To reduce distractions, sit with your feet on the floor.

Crossing your arms when hugging someone could be viewed as a protective gesture, implying that you don't want to talk about it. Extending your legs indicates that you are too relaxed to be cautious, and you may be invading another person's personal space at the same time. Crossing one's legs is more difficult for women due to the little area between their legs.

The head position and other indicators

The way you hold your head, the number of times you yeast, and even the frequency with which you breathe all reflect how interested you are in what you're saying. You must avoid appearing enthralled or bored by what is happening. People will undoubtedly provide the same courtesy to you if you demonstrate an interest in a specific area, increasing mutual respect. Breathing may be frequent and, at times, unnoticed. Excessive breathing implies that you are uneasy about the circumstance, and that others will feel similarly. Swallowing frequently is a bad habit since it implies uneasiness or disquiet. Scratching your temples also signifies that you are a quiet person.

Negative body language is an effective weapon for decreasing the self-esteem of others. These signals indicate any anxieties you may have and express to the audience that you are not being taken seriously; either you don't know what you're doing to the dialogue, or you don't know what you're doing to the dialogue. Excessive fidgeting, such as playing with one's clothes, face, or hair, indicates a lack of trust in the public. For example, asking for a raise at work, dealing with a difficult social circumstance, or even ending a relationship with a partner are all examples. If you want to be regarded seriously as a speaker or writer, your body language should support the worlds you create with your words. Respect is essential in practically every part of life and utilizing the appropriate phrases will assist you on your path to self-employment.

Verbal Language

The vocal component of communication includes all of the words you pick, as well as their comprehension and translation into other languages. Verbal communication refers to oral communication in which messages are communicated via spoken words. The transmitter communicates his or her feelings, impressions, concepts, and opinions to others through lectures, speeches, interviews, and discussions.

Accent, voice understanding, speech speed and pace, body language, and the coherence of the words used in the debate are all aspects that influence verbal communication efficacy. Feedback is instantaneous in verbal correspondence since both the sender and the recipient communicate and receive the message at the same time.

The sender's tone of voice should be loud and clear throughout the message, and the subject matter should be matched to the intended audience's interests and needs. The sender can contact the recipient at any time to ensure that the message is received and understood correctly. These types of interactions are more likely to be incorrect since words may not always properly convey a person's ideas and emotions.

Verbal communication success is determined not just by one's ability to talk, but also by one's capacity to actively listen. The speaker's capacity to listen to the topic matter is important to the success of a speech. Verbal interaction is appropriate in both professional and informal settings. Almost every career requires the capacity to communicate verbally. As a result, when determining who to hire, many job interviews place a high importance on linguistic proficiency.

The greater your listening abilities are, regardless of the profession for which you are seeking, the more likely you are to be hired. You will shine in both the interview and on the job. However, when there is little or no nonverbal communication to aid in message interpretation, the use of words is just as crucial, if not more important, in delivering the information.

Chapter 16
Getting to Know Yourself

This chapter will go through many ways for self-evaluation. To begin, we'll discuss the significance of self-awareness and why it's critical to spend time to it right away.

Simply described, self-awareness is the consciousness of one's own existence. Our distinctiveness is what sets us apart from others. Each of its several dimensions includes experiences, thoughts, and abilities. Psychologists discovered that focusing only on oneself enables us to examine and compare current conduct to previously held ideas and norms. As we move through life, we gain the ability to be self-aware and impartial assessors of our behaviors in respect to our fundamental ideals.

Remember that self-awareness includes our perception of our inner environment as well as noticing things in our own bodies. Have you ever undertaken a self-evaluation, based on your beliefs or experiences, for example? How may we begin to work toward this goal if non-judgmentalism is a necessary component of self-awareness? As we grow more aware of what is going on within us, we may be able to recognize and embrace them as inherent human characteristics. We shouldn't be too hard on ourselves if we make a few blunders. It's important to keep this in mind while you attempt to boost your self-esteem and confidence, because making mistakes is an unavoidable part of the process.

As stated in the opening chapter of this book, your ability to change your skills, particularly your capacity for strength, is heavily reliant on your ability to control your thoughts and emotions. As a result, you must communicate with your own personal views and ideals, often known as core values in another context.

Take a look at your current personal beliefs. Self-awareness is critical in this instance. To recognize your own views and beliefs, you must be able to reach your consciousness. Only once we've discovered which ideas are harmful to us and those, we want to change will we be able to change them.

How to Restore Your Connection to Your Core Values

If you contact your fundamental convictions, you will be able to become more assertive since you will be able to discuss your underlying principles and ensure that your criteria are met.

Understanding how to listen to your emotions is critical for understanding your own fundamental concepts. We live in a world where multitasking and dealing with distractions take precedence overpaying attention, going inward, and realizing one's deeper self. This is mostly due to media and consumerism, as information is constantly aired. Brief concentration intervals of a few minutes that allow a person to settle in for a short period of time may be rather delightful in this scenario. Reflection and engagement with your sensations will require significant work and devotion on your behalf, but it will become easier as you get used to it. This self-awareness will enable you to express yourself assertively in interpersonal interactions. You won't be able to do this until you have a firm grasp on your emotions, wants, and fundamental concepts.

Along with paying attention to your emotions, another way to connect with your inner principles is to pay attention to the deeper requirements that your senses may be signaling.

For example, if you have an emotion and withdraw, you can claim that you were deceived by someone else. Following that, you'll need to determine the underlying value or deeper need each feeling is associated with. Spend some time by yourself determining which obligations contravene your personal code of behavior.

For example, a close friend may reveal someone in whom you had confided, leaving you feeling betrayed. If you find yourself in this situation, you should ask yourself, "What is an unsatisfied personal need?" As the betrayed party, you have numerous alternatives available to you, and you must decide if they are necessary or desirable. Because you cherish friendship, you may feel betrayed if you realize that a buddy has lied to you. Furthermore, you may demand or value personal security, and your safety may be jeopardized in this case.

When you identify that you are having a negative emotion in a circumstance, you might think on it to see if you have any unmet personal needs or worth in that situation. Assessing your fundamental thoughts and beliefs will help this process. You'll have a better understanding of your values throughout time, and you'll discover which ones are most important to you at any particular time.

After determining your requirements and convictions, you may communicate calmly and assertively so that your desires and values are honored by both you and others, regardless of the situation.

Reconnecting with your core principles has numerous advantages.

Consider some of the most important qualities of your relationship. It could be a friendship, a romantic relationship, or a family bond. You respect character traits such as integrity, reliability, loyalty, and honesty. All of these characteristics demand the presence of a powerful person. It demands the presence of someone who can be trusted and acts in accordance with their principles and convictions, even when it is easier to let people go. This is where assertiveness comes into play because you must speak out for yourself in order to care for yourself and your needs. You can benefit from these ideas if you understand them and don't break them.

Your Individual Vision

In this regard, we will research your vision on your behalf. We'll begin by distinguishing between a vision and a goal. Many people confuse them because their goals and points of view are so similar.

To improve your outcomes and the outcomes of this section's goal planning technique, attempt to visualize the positive changes that will occur in your lives. For the sake of clarity, let us discuss the distinctions between a person's vision and his or her aim.

A person's vision does not need to be created from scratch; it already exists within them. Your self-perception as a forceful, self-assured individual who protects himself by sticking to his beliefs and opinions exemplifies this. A person's vision is a comprehensive picture of the goals they wish to attain as well as the long-term consequences of those goals. When individuals think about it, it represents the most essential aspects of that person's life in their minds, and it is frequently exciting, thrilling, invigorating, and full of varied wonderful feelings.

A vision, on the other hand, differs fundamentally from a goal. Everything that is intended intentionally and carefully to carry out a series of actions in order to accomplish a stated conclusion (the endpoint) is regarded a goal in the framework of goal setting.

While connecting with your own vision may seem difficult at first, I tell you that it already exists within you and that all you need to do is bring it to light. This will help you visualize a better version of yourself. Low self-esteem frequently leads to an erroneous negative opinion of oneself, which can cause a person to feel completely cut off from their vision. Visualization is an effective method for envisioning yourself and attaining your goals.

To begin, choose a spot that is calm and devoid of distractions. This may be the most difficult thing for you at first, but with practice, it will become easier and more natural. Once you've established this mindset, start imagining yourself as your ideal self. How does this version appear? What sets this version apart from others? What powers or skills does it have? How does this version appear? Make a concerted effort to consider all aspects of this version of yourself. You'll begin to picture your ideal self and future when you do this, and you'll be able to set goals to assist you get there.

How confident are you?

This part allows you to measure your current level of assertiveness and compare it to where you wish to be in the future. To begin, we'll discuss the various levels of stamina that people possess.

Extremely assured

If you are naturally aggressive, you will be able to defend yourself in practically any scenario, skillfully handle disagreements, and attain your goals while being true to your principles.

Incredibly Combative

You can have whatever you want if you are extremely powerful, but only if you consider the desires and sentiments of others.

Passive-Aggressive

If you're passive, it means you're continuously repressing your emotions, whether they're grief or wrath. When you reach your unavoidable breaking point, you will erupt in rage against whoever is in front of you.

Assertive

<u>Confidently assertive people share four qualities. The individuals' names are as follows:</u>

1. The most important thing is to raise your voice in a way that does not annoy or injure others.
2. Outline your preferences and selection criteria.
3. Confidence in one's capacity to react to situations and preserve interpersonal connections.
4. Effective communication skills

While some people are naturally more aggressive, as I indicated in the opening chapter of this book, aggression should be viewed as a fixed personality feature rather than a talent that can be learned and acquired through time.

What is the general public's perception of you?

Nonverbal communication indications and cues. It is vital to observe a person's body language in order to determine their emotional state.

Examining your own body language through the eyes of others can be quite beneficial in determining how others perceive you. When you connect with others, your body language conveys specific cues that influence how others view and perceive you. Others are constantly watching your body language to see how at ease you are or what you think about something. We'll look at some examples of body language to help you become more aware of the messages you're giving to others.

Closed body language refers to the presence of an individual who is isolated from the company of others with whom they are interacting. If you feel endangered, someone can cross his arms or clasp his fists together to shield you from the outside world. If you do, whether you realize it or not, you are physically striving to establish a barrier between yourself and yourself. Our bodies are alerted to the fact that they are under attack by our emotions and sentiments, and they respond appropriately. It doesn't matter if there is a genuine physical threat or if a topic of conversation makes us feel apprehensive about anything. Everything is the same to our brain.

The polar opposite of the above example, which we shall cover in greater detail later, is open body language. Relaxed body language, such as taking a comfortable seated position, relaxing back, and splashing around, or putting your arms out wide, can demonstrate your ease and safety in the connection. When someone feels at ease and pleasant, they are able to open their arms and receive the rest of the world.

It's more important to maintain track of how these body language cues change during interactions than it is to keep track of static verbal instructions, because this is when the most important learning occurs. Is the group quickly closing their eyes by putting anything between you and them, such as a notebook or a drink, or do they start shifting in their seats when the subject changes? Body language, particularly shifts in it, is critical for developing the ability to be an excellent listener and observer of the emotions of others. In most cases, nonverbal cues provide the majority of the information we obtain from an interaction.

It is critical to remember that nonverbal communication includes an important component that is frequently overlooked: what people do not say. When it comes to nonverbal communication, this is a challenging idea to grasp because it is viewed as a type of verbal communication in some circles. Nonetheless, because it does not require the use of words and is more of an abstract concept, it is classified as nonverbal communication.

It is just as vital to listen to what the other person (or individuals) has to say as it is to listen to what is ignored or excluded from the discourse. In other words, read between the lines. You can learn a lot about someone if they only talk about one item or avoids certain topics entirely. If we are not paying attention, we may not notice what they have left out or if they have stated crucial points or not. If you pay close attention and then examine the implications for you or your future thoughts and feelings, you can be confident that certain things have been avoided.

Using the examples above, you may start self-evaluating and examining your body language in a variety of situations. This reveals a lot about how other people perceive and view you.

As your communication style indicates

Examine your unique communication style and determine which mode of communication you use the most frequently using the definitions of the four basic types of communication in Chapter 2. We can mix and match different styles, but for the most part, we should stick to one. Determine the type of communicator you're dealing with using the descriptions. If you are dissatisfied with your most frequently used style, try not to be too hard on yourself and be honest with yourself. Throughout the rest of this book, you will discover how to communicate more successfully by employing an affirmative communication style.

What do you think of yourself?

Recognize your own sense of self-worth in order to better comprehend how others perceive you. This may assist you in determining whether you are afraid of success or believe you have no prospect of altering your life for the better.

Your overall self-esteem is determined by the sum of your individual self-esteem. If you have a high sense of self-esteem, you are confident in your talents and deserving of people's respect. If you have poor self-esteem, your views and opinions are more likely to be dismissed as unimportant. We'll start by talking about how to assess your self-esteem so you can decide where to start with your work.

Individuals who have poor self-esteem typically have their ideas and opinions overlooked or dismissed. You place a higher importance on your perceived shortcomings and previous failures than on your abilities, and you don't give yourself credit for them. Others are always more capable and successful than you, and you are always aware of this. Fear of failure keeps you stuck in a rut and prevents you from reaching your goals.

Examine the events that have taken place in your life. If you replied yes to at least four of the questions, you may have poor self-esteem.

- You've picked the wrong type of relationship.
- You're passing judgment on others.
- It's all up to you, but you're becoming too fixed in your ways.
- You've been humiliated, and you're at a loss for what to do. You're baffled.
- You're in a bad mood. You're in a bad mood.
- You're always worried

It's quite fine if you exhibit several of these symptoms. We'll look at a range of approaches to improve this later in the book.

Do you think of yourself positively?

The vast majority of people who have a healthy sense of self-esteem have a positive attitude about life. They have faith in their skills to succeed and do not waste time bemoaning their imperfections. You are not scared to seek assistance in order to reach your goals. They can also be confident, refusing to participate in situations or requests that make them feel uneasy.

Individuals who have a strong sense of self-worth live better lives because they focus on what they have accomplished and what they can do to achieve rather than their failings in the past or their fear of failure. In most cases, trust permits a person to develop in social situations, at work, in sports, and in other areas of life. Those with a healthy sense of self-worth devote their time and energy to pleasing themselves and delighting the rest of the world.

Below is a checklist of some of the indicators of a good self-image. Examine the ones that piqued your curiosity. According to the results, if you checked out fewer than four things on the quiz, you have low-medium self-esteem. If four or more of these boxes are checked, you have a healthy self-esteem that ranges between high and medium. You recognize and accept responsibility.

Do you have a positive self-image?

Many people hold the commonly held belief in self-esteem. According to this theory, some people exploit their high self-esteem to conceal their low self-esteem. Individuals who come into contact with this type of individual quickly see that they are dealing with someone who does not have a healthy sense of self-worth and should avoid them at all costs. Excessive self-esteem suggests to others that you do not respect yourself enough, and as a result, you must convey your qualities and abilities to others in order for them to grant you the respect you desire, and vice versa. This is referred to as overcompensation.

People with a strong feeling of self-worth are more inclined to conceal their lack of confidence. They exhibit symptoms that are distinct to those associated with poor self-esteem in order to conceal their low self-esteem.

People with low self-esteem, for example, are less likely to believe in themselves and, as a result, are less likely to use their skills to achieve their goals. Furthermore, those with exceptionally high self-esteem do not believe in or are self-conscious about their ability to fulfill their goals, preferring to spend an inordinate amount of time bragging about how much they accomplish and how good they are in order to appear trustworthy. You're aware of the difference, aren't you?

People who have a high sense of self-esteem are eager to extol their own majesty and superiority to others. Individuals, on the other hand, speak confidently while discussing a subject in which they have excelled. People with high self-esteem might exaggerate aspects of their lives in order to earn praise from others, while concealing their low self-esteem in other areas. "I believe in myself," for example, is a remark made by someone who has a high self-esteem. "After three years of half-marathon training and two failed tries, the event was finally completed yesterday. My marathon preparation has begun, and I plan to run for the next six months." A person with healthy self-esteem is able to express themselves and the task they have successfully completed without fear of failure. Their reactions are divided into two categories: severely unfavorable and extremely positive.

Those who have a strong sense of self-worth, on the other hand, may express themselves in the following ways: "I spent a year training for the half marathon. I'm prepared to bet that the entire marathon will be less difficult than most people believe!" The distinction in this remark is that the person does not acknowledge to failing and encountering hurdles along the path, which was unavoidable and comparable to other people's experiences. Instead of focusing just on their own objectives, they evaluate what it takes to teach others and how they might do so more efficiently and effectively.

People with an abnormally high feeling of self-worth may exhibit the following behaviors. Examine the ones that piqued your curiosity. You decline to take part in events or opportunities that appear to be too "simple" or outside of your skill set. You take on an excessive amount of work despite the fact that you know you won't be able to finish it all.

As a result, you notice a developing schism between yourself and some of your friends, which you blame on your arrogance. You see that some employees are hesitant to come to work, which you attribute to your extreme caution while doing your job. You are more concerned with your own abilities and performance, and you make no effort to include your spouse.

It's absolutely fine if you only glance at a few of them! Your strong self-esteem is probably certainly a result of your low self-esteem. After you've done your self-evaluation, you can investigate how you perceive yourself and how that perception influences your life, such as your capacity to make desired changes and express yourself more successfully.

How to comprehend something that may be useful to you

In addition to being aware of one's own existence, self-awareness necessitates paying great attention to one's own inner state and level of well-being with an open mind and heart. Your mind is incredibly capable of storing information and memories, including memories of our most common reactions to a wide range of life situations. These recollections serve as a reminder of how we are now feeling. Finally, knowing this information encourages our minds to react similarly in similar situations in the future.

When we acquire self-awareness, we can become aware of how our thoughts are conditioned and taught. Understanding this is the first step toward deprogramming your mind and teaching it new responses to future events. This is particularly useful during times of conflict or tension, when you want to improve your confidence but are having difficulty responding assertively due to stress or anxiety. If you are conscious of your own acts, you will be able to change your activities and become more assertive in your approach.

People who are self-aware are also more likely to act proactively rather than passively, and they have a greater level of mental well-being and a good outlook on life. The qualities and benefits of self-awareness were studied in a 2016 scientific study. They determined that three characteristics constitute self-awareness: attentiveness, insight, and self-reflection. People experience more acceptance and less emotional stress as a result of these characteristics. According to the study's findings, self-consciousness is a crucial characteristic for individuals aiming to be effective business executives who must retain discretion.

So, why should you care about your own self-awareness? Psychologists believe that self-awareness is the most significant factor in developing emotional intelligence. It's vital to be able to track and regulate your thoughts and feelings on a minute-to-minute basis if you want to better understand yourself and work intentionally to improve your communication, reaction, and interaction with others.

Chapter 17
Emotional Intelligence

Emotional intelligence has long been a source of contention. The idea that emotional intelligence should be increased is a well-worn path for both firm executives and rank-and-file personnel. Everything is determined by one's emotional intelligence.

Others, on the other hand, believe that emotional intelligence may be learned. Predictably, the author believes that the vast majority of us fall towards the latter type. However, in order to properly establish oneself through emotional knowledge, the following measures should be taken.

You'll learn how to evaluate a room's ambiance.

You've almost certainly overheard someone inquire about the temperature of the room. In this scenario, it is more vital to monitor the emotional condition of persons in close proximity than it is to check the room temperature, hence assessing the room temperature is less critical.

Is the intensity of your feelings high? Is it possible they've been apprehended? When you enter a room, there are a few basic ways to assess the general condition of all the emotions in the room. When you hear yelling and fighting, you know you've got some ill folks on your hands. Things, on the other hand, are frequently more complicated and sophisticated.

Consider the following scenario: you're chatting with someone you know. You should have a rough idea of what constitutes a "neutral arrangement" of all the actors in this situation. You should be able to distinguish who is calm and who isn't if you're surrounded by friends or other peers with whom you're familiar and speaking.

Is their facial expression neutral, as it should be in this situation? If not, what are some common, neutral terms you would use instead? Doubt? Worry? Anxiety? Frustration? Are they tense, swaying in their seats? Seeing someone who appears to be ordinarily calm and collected respond in this manner is a clear indication that something has gone wrong. If you can read the emotional temperature of a room, you will be better ready to cope with yourself.

It may be strange to suppose that we are fully unaware of our emotional state. After all, aren't we the ones in control of our emotions? We are the ones who are directly experiencing everything that happens in our lives, so shouldn't we be able to grasp how we feel better than anyone else?

Regardless of how reasonable everything looks to be, this is not always the case. Consider the situation of a driver who appears agitated and aggressive. The driver appears agitated, but when advised to calm down, he yells, "When you say, "cool down," what precisely do you mean?

In other cases, we are utterly unaware of our own feelings while they occur. We could even point the finger at others to explain our own concerns. For example, someone may appear dissatisfied, while the other person may be blamed for the commotion. To overcome this obstacle, we must learn to take deep breaths, take a step back, and focus on our feelings. Allow us a minute to reflect on how we felt at the time before making any important decisions or prepared to fight for an extended amount of time.

Recognize the influence you have on others.

Every person is an emotional creature, and the individuals we deal with influence our emotions. For example, if someone around begins to laugh, we are compelled to join in. In contrast, if someone is depressed and sobs in our presence, we may only be beginning to perceive their anguish. As a result, we communicate with one another through both words and emotions, both of which have a substantial impact on how we act and interact with one another.

In order to grow oneself through emotional intelligence, it is critical to be aware of how our emotions may affect others. For example, if you're having a horrible day and tell your wife that nothing is going right for you and that your entire existence is meaningless, this emotional assault may have an effect on her thinking.

Remember that your spouse is a member of the aforementioned "bunch of garbage," and they will begin to wonder if they will fail as a result of your displeasure. Something similar happened to me many years ago, but it was a long time ago. "Nothing made me happy," I said to my partner during a particularly gloomy period in our relationship, when I had just graduated from high school and was aimlessly drifting through life.

Due to my complete lack of emotional intelligence, I was able to persuade someone to reassess their entire relationship with me by making a single simple comment. We have the potential to either depress or stimulate others' emotional responses. This emphasizes the significance of communicating our emotions to others as opposed to simply notifying them of their inaction. Even though we want to be open, we must accept responsibility for how we express our emotions. Emotional intelligence is necessary to establish oneself.

Chapter 18
Handling Negative Comments

Everyone understands how difficult it is to be unable to find emptiness in their thoughts when what they truly require is a razor-sharp answer that is appropriately tailored to the occasion. It's one of those tasks you'd prefer avoid at all costs, but it always appears when you least expect it. Wouldn't it be great to be clever, quick, and funny at all times, regardless of where you are or what you're doing?

It's past time to hone the skill of responding to harsh remarks and insults with humorous retorts. In the sections below, we'll teach you ten different ways to utilize caustic language to train your friends, parents, coworkers, random strangers on the street, and even your dog.

You probably remember the annoying sentiment, picture what you may have said, and think how the unpleasant person would have appeared if you had that or that spectacular reaction in mind at the time. In general, there are times when you can unwind and reevaluate your circumstances. When ideal reciprocations, such as "If I had only spoken that," occur to the mind, there is nothing that can be done because it is already too late.

You must study subjects that will allow you to fill your thoughts with hundreds of possible responses to each situation in order to entirely eradicate this obstacle.

Answering questions necessitates a high level of nuance. It is vital not only to know what to say at a certain time, but also to say it correctly and successfully represent oneself. It is more important to understand the foundations for what others have to say than it is to understand the tactics that will assist you in finding an amazing answer.

When you combine all of these attributes, you obtain an unequaled ability to maintain your guard without exerting any effort on your behalf.

This collection contains no pre-written pieces or "packaged items." The most effective way to develop the kind of snappy reactions that politicians need to tell the truth is to utilize your emotions to learn from the responses of others. Believe me when I say you'd miss the perfect occasion to fire your verbal bullet because you'd spend much too much time each time wondering, "What response should I use?"

This chapter, on the other hand, will educate you about spontaneity, which is necessary for creating natural, startling, and creative reactions. If you're ready to master the art of the smart comeback, go over the information below and get started.

1. Even if these are unfavorable remarks about your shortcomings, they are usually made out of fear or concern for your job security. Some people do this when they are feeling down in order to improve their social standing. If you listen to anything else, you will be constantly in a bad emotional state, which will hinder your ability to be creative and generate beautiful sentences. You can answer to the other person's claims promptly and reasonably because to the distance between you and them. Keep in mind that anything spoken by others is simply that: words! In general, people do not intend what they say and act just for the reasons listed above. Accept this truth, as well as your own flaws, and keep in mind that no one has the power to make you feel awful without your permission.
2. To avoid taking things personally, you must maintain a condition of serenity, peace, and tranquility; this is the only mental state in which strong responses are natural and unavoidable. Furthermore, responding angrily to someone disqualifies your comment from consideration for the platform. Consider a worried person who is attempting to manage his or her stutter and perspiration! This would never happen, and the unlucky person would be made fun of as a result. Say what you need to say with composure and serenity, and it will come out correctly.
3. Maintain a somber demeanor when responding. 3. Try not to laugh while you're talking. Seriousness heightens the effect and makes the entire experience far more enjoyable for those who take part. Serious jokes are frequently more engaging

than lighter jokes. Act, and a horrifyingly serious response arises out of nowhere.

4. Almost certainly, you witnessed an outburst of laughing in reaction to someone's appropriate remark. This is not uncommon. Laughter fits are frequently generated as a result of something completely unexpected.

5. Make a connection to the season's most popular issue or fashion trend. All you have to do is keep up with the most essential events occurring across the world and in our own country. With so many scandals and odd or humorous circumstances in our society, it's easy to predict how people will react when a politician or celebrity irritates them. There is a plethora of options available. You can get a feel of what's on most people's minds right now by watching the news (though I wouldn't recommend doing so on a regular basis!), or you can follow such problems more casually online.

6. Take advantage of framing. It is one of the most effective NLP tactics since it takes a completely different approach to the same problem. Reframing is classified into two types: content reframing and context reframing. To elicit a favorable reaction, the question "What other, positive significance could this particular event have?" must be posed during content editing. In terms of reframing, you must respond to the following question: "Under what other conditions would this event be considered positive?"

7. "Without a doubt, this is my favorite story of all time!" You may encounter someone who is extremely talkative; they may begin to explain what you did wrong or how you should act, and you may find yourself unable to see a way out of their criticism. This is the time to get into your monologue, especially at the start: "Oh, absolutely, I adore the narrative!" You must say this with a broad grin and wide-eyed joy in your eyes, as though you truly appreciate what you're hearing and seeing. It will deafen your critics. If you're with a larger group (at least a few people), this gives you the opportunity to turn to others and say, "Listen closely; it's absolutely fantastic!" This frequently results in additional pressure and the annihilation of your detractors.

8. "We're talking about shoelaces," number eight says. If your speaker begins to talk about or listen to anything you don't want to talk about or hear, you can abruptly change the subject to something completely different and unexpected. Change the conversation to something related to the topic that this individual was about to bring up, but in an entirely other direction. Consider the following hypothetical scenario: "The pants you're wearing are inappropriate for your footwear," someone observes. "Have you heard of the Guinness World Records' record for the world's longest shoelace?" you ask. "Speaking of shoes, would rubbing black shoe polish on your bald head make it gleam like a diamond?" "Would your bald head shine like a diamond if I rubbed black shoe polish on it?" or "Would your bald head shine like a diamond if I rubbed black shoe polish on it?"
9. Have fun with yourself and others. Use witty retorts to de-stress, entertain yourself and others, or simply improve the tone of the occasion. This should not be done in an unpolitical or hostile manner, since this will only lead to uncomfortable arguments, which may later evolve into something far worse. When your remarks cause another individual to disagree, the best course of action is to either mute or ignore them. Even when confronted with the greatest response of the year (or century), someone who is truly proficient at the quick response knows when to call a halt to the dialogue. I understand how difficult it is to end something entertaining and precise but believe me when I say that swallowing words and holding them until a more appropriate time is preferable.
10. Use this ability only if you are convinced that the recipient will accept it with a smile or, at the very least, a cheerful temperament. Enjoy it, let your imagination go free, and astound everyone around you, but be cautious. These "magic bullets" eliminate the following: I promised you at the start of this chapter that I wouldn't provide you pre-written responses or "packaged knowledge," but here is an exception. These statements enable you to respond to anything someone says to you while still allowing you to

ponder and regain your calm. The following are the sentences that always begin with "It's intriguing":
- What gives you the impression that you're about to say anything like that?
- This is quite appealing. What will the focus of your queries be?

With these phrases, you won't be able to answer to anything.

They also drive others away as a result of their experiences, forcing them to confront their own stupidity, insignificance, and vanity. They have the capacity to persuade their interlocutors to think about their genuine intentions and the reasons for what they've told you and thrown at you. They either give up or immediately adopt a significantly more sympathetic approach. They can also function as a "wake-up call" under specific settings.

11. Assess your abilities. Your inner conversation, which is always making observations about the outside world, can be really valuable. For a few minutes, resting in a lovely, calm spot and interacting with your own thoughts may suffice. If, on the other hand, you do not want your family to consider obtaining psychiatric assistance, you should constantly practice in your thoughts. For success, you'll need two inner voices: one from a friend and one from yourself.

Imagine this person saying something hurtful, harsh, or insulting to you to complete the homework. The method is straightforward then you craft a smart, timely, and one-of-a-kind response. Of course, it may take a few minutes or longer at first to develop these responses, but conversing with one's own thoughts is not unusual, considering that practically everyone on the planet does it on a daily basis. You will progress in whatever time frame is required with practice and repetition. Allow your inner voice to say something horrible to you after you've gotten to your feet. Positive responses will occur more frequently and consistently with time.

Once you've mastered the aforementioned abilities, you'll be able to do verbal juggling feats. When the situation calls for it, retorts as sharp as a Japanese katana sword will spring from your mouth. Improve your capacity to discern acceptable reactions, and it will become second nature to you over time. Best wishes and have a wonderful time!

Chapter 19
Stop Apologizing All the Time

You are over-apologizing, despite the fact that you are not required to say, "I'm sorry." This can occur if you make a mistake, accept responsibility for another person's error, or accept responsibility for something you did not cause or control.

A couple of examples show excessive apologizing.

- If the waitress serves you the incorrect order, apologize and say, "Please accept my heartfelt apologies," adding, "I wasn't ordering it."
- You apologize to the receptionists at the doctor's office, saying, "I apologize for disturbing you." "I'd want to ask you a question," I say.
- If the store clerk accidentally spills your eggs, another employee will come out and fetch you another carton. "I'm sorry it took so long," you apologize to the individuals in front of you in line.
- Your partner makes a racially insensitive remark, which is promptly rejected. "Please accept my heartfelt apologies." "He/she isn't normally like this," you tell your buddies.
- In a meeting, behave as if you're apologizing profusely: "I'm very sorry." What causes our overshadowing, and why is it a problem?

As a result, why are so many of us so down on ourselves?

The following are some hypotheses as to why this is happening.

- Appealing to a diverse group of people. You have earned the right to be called pleasant and thoughtful. You're concerned about how others perceive you, and you're determined not to offend or mislead them in any way.
- A lack of self-esteem. You have low self-esteem and are concerned that you have made a mistake, such as meeting

- difficulties, obstructions, irrationality, or unrealistic expectations.
- Obsessive-compulsive disorder (OCD) (obsessive-compulsive disorder). You set such lofty objectives for yourself that you will never be able to meet them. As a result, you're constantly self-conscious and feel forced to apologize for something you've done incorrectly.
- You recognize your own self-consciousness. We deeply regret being nervous or insecure, as well as not knowing what to do or say in particular situations. As a result, we justify ourselves and everyone who tries to console us.
- You are responsible for the conduct or omissions of others, including your own. For example, a relationship partner may apologize as though they were at fault for their spouse's conduct (such as being late or interrupting). It's possible that you're acting as a single entity rather than as two independent people. You are not liable for the decisions made by the people with whom you live or are married. Accepting responsibility and apologizing for their behavior just serves to perpetuate their problematic behavior by relieving them of the burden of accountability.
- It's a shabby custom. If you have been overly excusing yourself for a long time or have heard others do so, you are likely to do so unknowingly. It was a reflexive reaction that came completely out of nowhere. Apologies are no different. Excessive apologies erode sympathy at the most inopportune time. Excessive apologies will also impair your future hopes. You may believe you are sorry for everything — for your choices and emotions, for space, for being alive — but you are not. Insensitive apologies such as "I'm sorry," "I'm wrong," or "I'm guilty" are a subliminal method of admitting responsibility for one's actions. This does not imply that you are confident or deserving.
- For co-dependents, over-apologizing is a common source of distress. This is due to our low self-esteem, fear of disagreement, and laser-like attention on the wants and feelings of others. We also have fragile constraints that are

frequently interconnected, allowing us to carry responsibility for actions we are unable or unwilling to manage. We also recognize our obligation to aid others in addressing or conquering their problems. We are accountable for their conduct as if they were our own. We believe that we are entirely responsible for everything that occurs, a belief that most of us have had since childhood. We are quite aware that we are causing annoyance or difficulty to others. We are terrified of rejection and criticism; therefore, we go to great lengths to make others feel at ease around us.

A list of activities that you should absolutely discontinue

- Unless you are perfect, you will occasionally make excuses in life (and no one is). Furthermore, two simple words — "I'm sorry" — might have far-reaching consequences.
- According to studies, making excuses allows us to avoid the humiliation of wrongdoing others while also repairing trust between the two parties.
- It can also help us maintain our dignity by increasing our trust in trustworthy sources as well as our faith in our own spiritual goodness and goodness.
- However, just as too much sugar is unhealthy for you, so is too much "my evil." According to Deborah Tannen, a Georgetown University professor of linguistics and author of the book You Just Don't Understand, excessive apologies may create the appearance of a lack of attention and competence.

Among the most well-known instances are:

"Women who continuously apologize may be quite happy," she notes, "but they are frequently overlooked for promotions because they do not appear to be qualified for the post." "After refusing to accept responsibility, they are regarded as excessively hostile.

According to Juliana Breines, a doctoral student and assistant professor of psychology at the University of Rhode Island, severe self-criticism could be the culprit. "Excessive apologies leads to people being unduly harsh on us or condemning us for our flaws," the author continues, rather than acknowledging that everyone makes errors, and no one expects you to be flawless.

She claims that when people are humiliated or guilty of their acts, they may apologize for other people's assurances, even though the person for whom they apologize suffered no harm as a result of their activities.

While this is correct, it does not diminish the importance of recognizing our errors and making restitution when we are clearly at fault. Even if we are not sorry, we always say, "I'm sorry." "Would you kindly accept my heartfelt apologies?"

Make a mental note if you can connect: these two sentences aren't the most effective techniques to relieve stress, maintain a cheerful countenance, or demonstrate empathy.

When you're going to do anything, don't offer an excuse for any of the seven reasons listed below. If you are unable to drink in your original tongue, use one of the alternate phrases.

1. Your thoughts

Every friendship demands a commitment to communicate one's thoughts and ideas with the other. By sharing your feelings to the other person, you assist them understand you. Donna Flagg, author of Surviving Difficult Conversations, recommended individuals to "own it." The argument isn't that if you have a strong urge, you should fully express it. If you have unresolved childhood injuries, don't bring them up at the Thursday conference. Despite the fact that it is prohibited, Flagg believes that the argument "I'm furious by this" or "I'm upset with..." is completely reasonable. This also applies to Breines' claim that he is "overly sensitive" while appealing for compassion. We devalue ourselves when we apologize for being offended or enthused about something in an inadequate attempt to defend someone. For example, "I'm sorry" may be replaced by "I get irritated when..."

2. Use of the internet.

According to Breines, when we apologize for being tired, having a horrible hair day, or dressing in an unflattering manner, we are actually displaying a lack of self-compassion. "Could you please explain why you're so sorry to be here?" You should not try to change your identification or how you want to wear your hair today unless you are wearing sweatpants and a food-fed t-shirt, or unless you are expressly violating the dress code for a specified purpose. Instead of apologizing, say nothing. Establish your physical presence.

3. Me time

Each individual requires a certain amount of personal space in order to function properly during the day. People suffering from anxiety, for example, may require more. As a result, seeking mental breathing space is crucial for our mental health, even if it means disconnecting from a friend for a workout or a date. According to Flagg if you're unwilling to take "me time," you're definitely overthinking things. Requesting a rain check is worthless if all you want to do is see the person you've cancelled on. What if the individual with whom you're chatting becomes enraged? She believes that your public declaration of a desire for isolation is motivated by their anxieties rather than your own. Instead of apologizing, say something like, "Today, I actually need relaxation." You may also say something like, "This evening, all I need is stillness for me." "I need to be alone," you could remark.

4. Explaining questions

By apologizing for wanting a challenge, we make ourselves look silly. Anyone can do this to protect their egos from a coworker or acquaintance who rolls their eyes or chews on their abilities. "However," Flagg recommends, "whether you seek aid or an explanation, you should resist feeling compelled to apologize." If the interrogation is examined, it may be discovered that he suffers from personal anxiety concerns. Instead of apologizing, try this: "Could you perhaps assist me in making sense of this?" "Could you please explain it a bit further?"

5. The most desirable location

Prior to being exposed to someone who badly abuses them, their behavior was utterly out of control (e.g., organizing a date with two pals that you assumed they would get along only to learn one of them was a genuine jerk). As a result, Flagg believes an apology is unnecessary. If we say the same thing to someone we encounter in a store or on the street, we apologize. "Some people feel forced to apologize and may even assume they are to fault when the other person does not apologize," adds Breines. If you are one of those people who can't help but respond in certain situations, consider substituting a more self-loving answer.

    6. You must respond immediately to a tweet, phone call, or email

We may not always be able to personally respond to a family member or coworker. Apologizing for taking longer than a split second to reply, according to Flagg, creates a problem with something that should not have been a problem unless there was an emergency (which is almost always the case). It may also convey the impression that our own ambitions are secondary to those to which we respond. Flagg quickly approves the query and then informs you of what else is on the table in order to prevent caving in if there are too many individuals waiting for you right now. People can be certain, according to Flagg, that they are aware of the environment they have produced.

    7. You cannot change the situation, and you have to accept that. You're well aware that the automatic answer when presented with a nagging lawyer, an unsanitary boss, or someone in a toxic relationship is "I'm sorry." Rather than adding to the problem's challenges by verbalizing a difficulty, she delivers the political cure, "That'll be exceedingly uncomfortable" or "That'll be extremely difficult for you." You don't seem to be able to keep the s-word out of your vocabulary. Tannen recommends adding a couple more sentences, such as "I'm deeply sorry this happened." This way, you don't come across as blaming yourself for something absolutely beyond your control.

Chapter 20
Stress and Anxiety Management

At some point in everyone's lives, stress affects nearly every part of their lives. What you're experiencing is your body's reaction to whatever has occurred or is occurring at the time. Your body reacts to disease in several ways, including physical, behavioral, and emotional stress.

Indeed, stress is one of the processes by which the body helps us escape danger. It can also improve your productivity and ingenuity. Even happy life events, such as starting a family, getting married, or having a new child, can bring stress. While stress does have certain benefits, persistent or severe stress is another matter. Some people suffer tension and worry as a result of expecting unfavorable scenarios. People will believe they are being watched and that decisions are being made for them if they get a continuous impression that they are being followed and that decisions are being made for them.

This is exceedingly risky because it can result in potentially fatal physiological, behavioral, and emotional difficulties. We might discuss the harmful effects of stress, how it affects communication, and the most effective stress management methods.

Stress's impact

The body's reaction to stress sets off a chain reaction. Your heart rate may speed up, your blood pressure may rise, your breathing may become shallower, and your muscles may tighten. The body prepares to react as soon as possible if at all possible.

Stress can cause symptoms to spread throughout a person's body. It can have major or long-term effects on one's health, social life, and behavior. As an example of a potential indicator, consider the following:

- Stomach pains, diarrhea, constipation, and nausea
- Muscle spasms and soreness are two of the most typical signs of muscle spasms.

- Insomnia or other sleep-deprivation symptoms
- Energy exhaustion
- Migraine headaches and migraines
- anxiousness or tremors
- Immune system function has deteriorated.
- Excessive salivation
- Teeth grinding or tightened jaw
- Near-death suffocation
- Consistently sweating

Chronic stress can cause a heart that is underdeveloped, high blood pressure, and irregular heartbeats. Stress can trigger heart attacks and strokes, and panic episodes can mimic the symptoms of a heart attack or stroke.

Long-term stress, among other things, can lead to weight gain, erratic eating habits, menstrual abnormalities, and respiratory difficulties. Constipation, IBS, peptic ulcers, and gastroesophageal reflux disease are all examples of digestive system diseases. Stress manifests itself emotionally as much as mentally.

Psychoneuroimmunology (PNI) is a field of immunology that investigates the link between the immunological and neurological systems. According to MentalHelp.net, "chronic stress can cause or exacerbate mood problems such as depression and anxiety, bipolar disease, cognitive (thinking) impairments, personality changes, and problem behavior."

Stress Communication

Communication is another method for transmitting strain. Stressed people are more inclined to become upset or enraged. Your capacity to communicate effectively will suffer as a result. When your emotions are running high, it may be difficult to choose your words carefully or communicate effectively in public. You feel compelled to separate and isolate yourself from your loved ones. When this happens, people lose communication with their family and are unable to get sufficient help and medical attention. When people are sad, they frequently misinterpret the motivations of others or the messages they are attempting to convey. Another way depression can interfere with communication is when it is necessary to give a public speech. As a result of the flight or fighting response, individuals are compelled to abandon the situation. While stress can be detrimental in a variety of ways, it is also manageable. Some stress-relieving techniques are listed below.

Causes of Stress

The first stage in stress management is determining the source of the issue. Perhaps you aren't aware of what is triggering your depression. It is possible to be tense without realizing why. This term can also refer to "stressful circumstances." The same problem, however, does not impact everyone. A person's job or studies may overwhelm him or her, whereas another may withdraw. Once you've identified your stressors and developed a solid strategy for dealing with them, you can begin to control your stress. Improve your communication skills with you. When we communicate ineffectively with others, we contribute to stress levels rising. No one is capable of relieving our stress at various points in our lives. However, there are times when we can relieve our stress by communicating.

1. Communication in the workplace and in school

Many people suffer from acute depression as a result of their jobs. You could anticipate feeling more worried when starting a new career as you learn new things and obtain new talents. If you've been at your job for a long time and your supervisor has unrealistic expectations, it may be time to speak out. Effective communication is required to maintain a safe working environment.

Although it is not always possible to maintain a pleasant working relationship with your boss, being under extreme stress is preferable. While your organization may not be able to alleviate your stress, it may be able to assist you in finding new ways to achieve your objectives.

Academics are exempt from this restriction in any way. If the subject you're studying is too challenging, speak with your lecturer. You'll be able to detect if you're actively seeking a mentor or someone to assist you during working hours.

2. Make connections with those you are associated with. 2.

Other people's connections are another major source of stress. The availability of social support and the quality of one's interpersonal relationships are both crucial variables in one's overall well-being. Our stress levels grow when we are under pressure with a girlfriend, roommate, family member, or close friend.

Communicating as soon as possible is one method for preventing unwanted contacts. If you're worried, rather than waiting for a break, inform a friend, family member, or acquaintance. You may de-escalate potentially hostile situations by expressing your rage or unhappiness in a political manner.

We should also be prepared to pay great attention while a loved one communicates his or her emotions.

3. Do not be concerned with stress in friendship, family, or love.
Finally, if you're feeling overwhelmed or dissatisfied by your life, talk to someone. Discuss with people the things that make you uncomfortable, as well as your emotions.

If you suffer from depression on a frequent basis, you should seek the advice of a licensed physician to help you cope. A UCLA study found that expressing your thoughts can help you feel less depressed, irritated, or in pain.

According to the primary author, Matthew D. Lieberman, "When you drive with your foot on the brake or see a yellow light, you appear to be putting the brakes on your emotional emotions... We can recuperate faster if we write down our emotions. We hope that by encouraging a depressed friend to talk about it, we would be able to help them feel better."

4. Additional techniques for eliminating redundancy
Stress reduction is also thought to be aided by healthy nutrition. Caffeinated beverages in excess can be damaging to the body and add to tension. Excessive use of alcoholic beverages, sugar, salt, and nicotine is also harmful.

Stress can be relieved by eating foods high in vitamin B, vitamin C, and magnesium. When the body is stressed, these nutrients help to restore life and strength.

It will also benefit from adequate rest, meditation, prayer, and relaxing activities such as taking a hot bath or receiving a massage. Another way to combat depression is to engage in hobbies or outdoor activities.

Keep a healthy level of stress.

While stress is an unavoidable aspect of life, it should not be dismissed. If you're always stressed, start with modest modifications that will make you feel better right away.

Allow yourself time to unwind, talk to friends, and remember to explain yourself clearly. These modest changes could be the start of a true transformation, freeing you from the burden you've been carrying.

Anxiety Communication

When a person is called to speak in front of a group, he or she becomes nervous, making communication difficult. Anxiety over communication is a legitimate concern, especially if you anticipate speaking in front of large people as part of your job.

Anxiety symptoms in connection with communication

Men and women communicate in different ways, but they all share one trait: a lack of faith, which leads to their apprehension of communication. Regardless of the underlying causes of their lack of confidence, a person who suffers from speech anxiety is concerned that something will go wrong during a discussion and that they will not be able to recover quickly. Concerns include increased heart rate and dyspnea, as well as reduced focus and a dry mouth. While cognitive-behavioral therapies (CBTs) can aid in the treatment of speech anxiety, you can also practice speaking about difficult events on your own.

If you are unable to communicate due to worry, make an attempt to better your circumstances. To begin, avoid interacting with hostile audiences wherever feasible. If you are asked to speak in the near future, you have no choice but to cooperate: Prepare for the challenge by taking the appropriate steps. It's difficult enough to talk in front of a crowd; don't make it any more difficult by having them misinterpret what you're saying. Planning ahead of time will help to alleviate communication anxiety.

Assume you're giving a speech to a group or an audience. Examine your physical look. Examine your physical look. Take a peek around at the people. Look for a swarm. Familiarize yourself with the sensations and allow your brain time to develop confidence before the circumstance arises. Because your mind is focused with the game, it will be easier for you to maintain your calm when speaking.

Recognize that you have communication anxiety and that you can forecast your symptoms throughout a conversation. Begin by taking calm, deep breaths and being gentle with yourself. After a few minutes, your heart rate should calm, and your other symptoms should subside.

Please keep in mind that your ability to adjust does not trump your anxiety. Show the audience how ecstatic you are. Make an attempt to appear excited: appearing pleased to others can help you feel less anxious. People will respond to your activities more positively if they know you are joyful rather than concerned.

Maintain your focus on the present moment. It is a mistake to allow your thoughts and the dangers that await you to drift into the future. Maintain your current position of authority.

Chapter 21
Anger Management

Failure to regulate your irritation can lead to a range of problems, including saying something you'll later regret, yelling at your children, upsetting coworkers, writing rushed letters, health problems, and even physical violence. However, not all eruptions are as intense. Rather, rage might be shown through time spent fretting about causing operational delays, being impatient in traffic, or missing work.

Managing your fury does not mean you will never be furious again. Recognizing your emotions, addressing your rage, and then redirecting your hatred into something constructive are all part of the plan. The ability to control one's fury is a skill that everyone should develop. Even if you believe you have a good handle on your fury, there is always space for improvement.

What is management, exactly?

Anger management encompasses a variety of techniques to assisting a person in dealing with their emotions, emotions, and attitudes in a safe and productive manner. Because unmanaged irritability typically leads to risky behavior, anger management encompasses a wide range of techniques to assisting a person in safely and productively coping with their emotions, emotions, and attitudes.

A methodology for understanding anger

Anger is a normal, healthy, well-balanced unpleasant emotion. It conveys a message that, like any other emotion, can be distressing, unjust, or destructive. The message will never be delivered if the initial outburst of wrath fails to communicate it. While it's understandable to be angry when you've been treated unfairly or tricked, anger becomes a problem when it manifests in a way that affects you or others.

You may believe that expressing your fury is acceptable, that those around you are too emotional, that your rage is justifiable, or that expressing your rage is required to be respected. Wrath, on the other hand, is much more likely to destroy your reputation, impair your judgment, and impede you from growing in your career.

Anger's effects

When your fury becomes chronic, it can have disastrous repercussions. Health and well-being Health and well-being Workplace stress and rage have been related to a variety of health problems, including heart disease, diabetes, a weakened immune system, anxiety, and high blood pressure. It is critical to maintain excellent mental health. Chronic indignation impairs emotional talents and distorts perspective, making it difficult to focus and enjoy life. It can lead to tiredness, sadness, and other mental health problems.

- The workplace setting. Constructive criticism, innovative disputes, and spirited debate are all potentially beneficial. All you have to do is scrub your coworkers, managers, or clients, lowering their appreciation level.
- Interpersonal interactions Anger is the emotion that produces the most devastating meetings and relationships and leaves the deepest wounds. When you have an explosive temper, it is difficult for others to believe you, speak freely, or feel safe, which is especially problematic for youngsters.

If you have a poor temper, you may feel unable to handle the issue and calm the beast. You do, however, have more control over how you express your wrath than you realize. If you realize and address the underlying causes of your wrath, you may be able to learn to express yourself without disturbing others and keep your temper from taking over your life.

Anger myths and facts

Myth: I shouldn't have to "repress" my wrath. Everything works, so we can unpack and remove everything. Ventilation is as hazardous as managing and dispelling rage. To avoid wrath from erupting, it cannot be violently "let out." Outbursts and tirades, on the other hand, just feed the fire and aggravate an already perilous situation.

Myth: Rage, violence, and force assist me in identifying and obtaining what I need. Bullying from a third party is not permitted. People fear you, but they despise you if you can't maintain your cool under duress or deal with conflicting views. If you appear pleasant, people are more inclined to pay attention to you and meet your requirements.

Myth: I have no ability to save myself. I have no way of saving myself. Irritation is unavoidable and tough to manage. Even if you have little control over your surroundings or emotions, you do have some influence over how you express your wrath. It's also crucial to avoid being physically or verbally hostile when presenting your opinions. Even if someone pushes one of your buttons, you must describe your following steps.

Wrath is a strong emotion that can range from mild irritation to wrath. Indignation is sometimes perceived as a bad feeling, despite the fact that it may be extremely beneficial in certain circumstances. If you're filled with wrath, you could feel compelled to assist others or make a difference in their lives. Unchecked rage might appear as aggressive acts like shouts or property destruction. Furthermore, angry thoughts may cause you to disconnect from the rest of the world and focus completely on yourself, which can be detrimental to your health and well-being. When anger is experienced frequently or violently, when it is expressed improperly, and when it has a negative influence on one's physical, emotional, or social well-being, it is considered a problem. As a result, conflict resolution techniques can assist you in communicating your emotions in the most acceptable manner possible.

Anger management strategies

Several clinical trials have shown that cognitive-behavioral therapy can aid in dispute mediation. These treatments have the power to alter your beliefs and behaviors. Perceptions, emotions, and behaviors are all intertwined in this idea. Your senses and activities can either intensify or de-intensify your emotions. As a result, if you wish to avoid wrath, you must alter your words and behaviors. If you don't have access to oxygen, the fire within you will smolder and become more comfortable.

Only by using an anger management approach will you be able to learn to regulate your anger. If you get frustrated, you'll know just what to do. These tactics are intended to assist you in managing and controlling your fury.

1. Identification of triggers

If you've developed a good habit, make a note of the things that worry you. Long lines at the grocery store and in traffic, as well as scathing tweets and everyday wear and tear, can all cause you to lose your cool. While you can't blame anyone or anything for your inability to maintain your cool, knowing what gets you upset will help you prepare for it. Alternatively, before encountering potentially distressing events, you should practice conflict resolution techniques. By applying these strategies, you can increase your concentration and avoid getting distracted by a single unfavorable experience.

2. Evaluate your anger feelings

Consider whether your rage is a friend or an enemy before attempting to calm yourself. Whether you observe a violation of someone's rights or are a victim of abuse, your wrath may be beneficial. You could try to adjust your circumstances rather than relying exclusively on your emotional state in some situations. Rage could indicate that something else in your life, such as an emotionally manipulative or unhealthy relationship, needs to change.

However, if your wrath causes you discomfort or causes you to lose your temper in front of others, it may be regarded an opponent. According to the definition, feeling out of control and afterwards regretting your statements or acts are both indications of this type of rage. In these circumstances, it is appropriate to focus your attention on coping with your feelings and relaxing as much as possible.

3. Check for attendances and ensure you are up to date.

Perhaps you'll move from calm to furious in a matter of seconds. However, there are certain broad warning indications that your irritation is worsening. Recognizing these issues early allows you to take action and keep your irritation from increasing. Consider your physical manifestations of rage. Perhaps your heart rate increased, or your face warmed up. You'll also notice that your fist is tightening. There's a chance you'll notice changes in your neurology. You may experience dizziness or "see red." Knowing what to look for allows you to take decisive action to avoid doing something or doing something that may cause further problems.

4. Feeding your Anger

Trying to win an argument or maintain an unfavorable situation will simply feed your fury. When your level of frustration escalates, one of the wisest things you can do is to leave the situation right immediately. When a dispute becomes heated, it is best to take a pause. Take a walk if your children are causing you stress. A break can be beneficial to both the mind and the body in terms of relaxation. Explain to someone with whom you're having a heated argument, such as a friend or family member, the importance of pausing the topic and returning to it when you're feeling calm and collected. If you must take a break, make it a point to focus on controlling your anger rather than avoiding difficult situations. Once you've regained your composure, you should continue the conversation or reintroduce the subject. Scheduling a specific time and location to handle the problem is also advantageous. As a result, resolving the issue with your partner, colleague, or family member will be lot easier in the future.

5. Conversations between friends

It may be useful to discuss an issue or share your emotions with a supportive individual. It is vital to note, however, that venting will result in a reaction. Explicitly criticizing your supervisor, describing all of the reasons you detest them, or screaming about perceived injustices will just stoke the fire. One prevalent misconception is that you must express your anger in order to feel better. Experiments, on the other hand, demonstrate that you are under no obligation to "express your frustration." When you're angry, shattering things and throwing objects at people might amplify your rage. This indicates that employing this coping strategy should be done with caution. When conversing with a friend, ensure that you are focused on finding a solution or removing aggravation rather than whining. They are not intended to be a container for your thoughts. Instead, you may discover that shifting your attention away from your insane state of mind is the most effective way to employ this strategy. Anger manifests as a fierce anger outburst.

Physical activity is a simple way to capitalize on this increase. Exercise can help you cope with stress, whether it's a little walk around the block or a trip to the gym. Physical activity on a regular basis also aids in the decompression process. Aerobic activity will lift your spirits, allowing you to deal with wrath more effectively. Furthermore, training benefits your mind by purifying it. After a long or rigorous exercise, you'll have a better grasp of what was bothering you. Vacation time should be properly planned. Making a reservation at a nearby hotel can give you more control over your vacation.

Angry feelings increase the temperature of the fire. "I'm not sure how much longer I can put up with it," I think. As your aggravation rises, you'll think to yourself, "This traffic delay is going to spoil everything." When you're upset about anything, try to reframe your feelings. Instead, state the facts, such as "millions of automobiles are on the road every day," or something similar. There will be traffic bottlenecks on the highways from time to time." Keeping your cool and avoiding making doomsday predictions or exaggerating the situation can be accomplished by focusing on the facts. You can even make up a chant to recite to yourself to help you calm down. Using phrases such as "I'm alright." or "It's not nice, but..." It will assist you in either reducing or suppressing your anger.

An eruption of wrath results from ruminating over a terrible occurrence. After a very stressful day at work, for example, spending the entire night correcting everything that went wrong could be quite unpleasant. Changing the channel on your television and focusing on something else could be the most efficient method to unwind.

You can't always tell yourself, "Don't worry about anything," because life happens. Diverting your focus away from the task at hand is the most effective approach to shift gears physically throughout an operation. Do something that requires your complete attention, making it more difficult for unhappy or unpleasant sensations to enter your thoughts and feelings. Deep cleaning the kitchen, weeding the yard, paying bills, and playing with the kids are all time-consuming tasks. Maintain mental control so that you don't spend too much time thinking about what irritates you.

There are various techniques for calming down and letting go of frustration. Deep breathing exercises and progressive muscular relaxation are two stress-reduction strategies that are widely used. As a result, whether you're irritated at work or annoyed by an invitation to a meal, you can quickly and simply release your stress.

You may not trust them at first, or you may doubt that they are working for you. Before continuing, it might be beneficial to pause for a moment to consider the feelings that are feeding your wrath. Anger is frequently utilized as a defense mechanism against negative emotions such as guilt, despair, and dissatisfaction.

If you receive unfavorable feedback, for example, you may become frustrated since the situation makes you feel ashamed. If you are certain that the other person is incorrect in their assessment, it may be best for you to remove your humiliation as soon as possible. Recognizing the underlying emotions, on the other hand, will assist you in determining the basis of the problem. Then you'll have to make a decision on what you're going to do. If, for example, someone cancels your plans and your underlying emotion is loss rather than annoyance, you might consider how you wish to convey your feelings about the cancellation. In most cases, being outraged has the opposite consequence of pulling others away from you. Make a relaxation package that you may use to unwind when you get home from work and are disturbed by your family, or if you know the meeting at work is bothering you.

Consider purchasing goods that allow you to use all of your senses at the same time. You may alter your mood by exposing yourself to soothing sights, aromas, and tactile sensations. A cool-down box can include aromatic hand creams, photographs of quiet countryside, a spiritual reading passage, and a few of your favorite delicacies, among other things. Keep a supply of products that you know will keep you cool on hand.

You can put relaxing music and photos, as well as guided meditation and breathing technique instructions, on your smartphone by creating a separate folder for them. Many people assign meaning to their rage-filled outbursts. If you yell loudly enough at someone, they will comply with your wishes. While aggressive behavior may serve your short-term objectives, it has long-term effects that must be addressed. Even if your comments may not result in the immediate termination of a relationship, they can have a long-term impact.

Effective communication skills are essential to moderate one's rage.

At some point in their lives, everyone becomes outraged, and if they are unable to manage their wrath, they may talk or act recklessly, or even violently, damaging others. If, on the other hand, you choose to ignore your feelings, you will grow frustrated. According to Jeanne Segal, a psychologist and co-founder of HelpGuide.org, self-directed signs of violence include high blood pressure, high cholesterol, and despair. If you have good listening skills, you might be able to control your rage by learning to speak boldly rather than offensively.

Take a big breath before speaking to someone. If you're having difficulties relaxing, try employing a specific phrase or verb, such as "reassure" or "relax." Keep in mind that paying attention and remaining cool will enable you to make a more accurate assessment of the situation.

Maintain your concentration and take a step back. It's not your job to "understand" how people feel or why they make decisions. Consider your emotional reaction to the situation before making a reasonable decision about how to handle it. Because the emotional component has been removed, you may explain and rationalize your rage.

Instead of being rude, be forceful in your reaction. Use "I" phrases rather than ""you" r" expressions to underline your requirements. A confrontational person may respond to receiving a report that must be completed by Monday by responding, "You still do it with me." This puts the opposing party on the defensive and increases the already high level of hatred in the scenario. Instead, use your excellent listening skills to say something like, "I'm truly sorry, but I just received your request." Setting a timeframe is crucial because the investigation will not be completed until the end of the working day." Using this strategy, you can show the other person that you are listening and prepared to participate, but that the current situation does not satisfy your demands in a forceful yet polite manner. If at all possible, practice your vocabulary so that you feel comfortable engaged in hostile speech.

Overgrowth should be prevented at all costs. When conversing with people, avoid using the terms "always," "never," or "everyone." Instead of thinking "everyone benefits from my presence" and becoming even more furious during a debate, focus completely on the opposing side. Instead, say, "I'm sorry, but I won't be able to finish this for you over the weekend." This keeps the argument on track and prevents the wrath from escalating out of hand.

Nonverbal indicators can be used to indicate confidence. With the words you choose, you transmit a great deal of emotion. Use a confident, calm tone of voice. Simply put, you should be proud of yourself and look the other person in the eyes. Maintain a neutral tone on your lips. Please keep your hands on your hips at all times. Please remember this. According to the American Psychological Association, monitoring your physical reactions can help you cope with a stressful situation by allowing you to relax more, psychologically reframe the issue, and focus on the rational components of a difficult scenario.

Chapter 22
Be Assertive

We've all been on the receiving end of a "please, please" request at some point in our lives. We initially protested, but soon caved in and consented because we were under duress. No matter how many times we say no, anyone can approach us and beg us until we cave in. When they beg, we may feel terrified and enraged. We are unable to think clearly since we are aware that someone will continue to ask us for something. As a result, our performance and relationships may deteriorate as a result.

If we believe in our ability, we can firmly say no. We can communicate our point without being overly critical of ourselves. If we are self-assured, we can say no without fear of people pleading with us. Assertiveness necessitates taking a strong and positive stance in support of your own and others' ideals. Furthermore, as is typically the case in most situations, confidence does not necessitate accepting the untrue.

Confidence in communication is a crucial skill. It may enable you to stand up and express yourself without jeopardizing the beliefs or rights of others. While some people are born with confidence, it is possible to cultivate one's own. You must believe in your ability to be a nice person, because if you say no, you must mean it. If you want to preserve your power but avoid a conflict, this is the time to plant a corporate no without getting into a dispute.

If you succeed, you will have accomplished your aim without causing harm or difficulties to yourself or others. To be aggressive, you must have emotional intelligence to recognize when you may be offending people. For a moment, consider the distinctions between being silent, assertive, and assaultive. Individuals who are driven to please others, whether passive, aggressive, or aggressive, are more prone to bend their will to meet their expectations and demands. This means that they express their agreement to others orally, even if they do not agree. One example is consenting to something even when we know it is bad.

Individuals appreciate the fact that when they act assertively, others mistake their actions as aggressive. They feel that if they disagree with someone or their principles, they will be mocked and thrown out of the group. Passive people allow others to pass them by unnoticed. You don't stand up for what's right, whether it's for the sake of others or your own. Passivity implies that you are sacrificing your voice for the sake of those around you.

When one is viewed as being overly passive, it becomes more difficult to take oneself seriously. People can see straight through you and, as a result, do not trust you, even if you do and say exactly what you want them to do. Passive behavior can also have a negative impact on a person's self-esteem, confidence, and capacity to express oneself. Being forceful is being able to convey your message to others without upsetting them. It strikes the ideal blend between decency and toughness. When you're upset at someone, you don't become scarlet or "suck up."

Being overly honest could indicate that you're restricting your own development. Unless you are adamant about getting your point over, you will be unable to listen to or comprehend what others have to say. You are unable to sympathize with others since you are personally involved. Being inactive may be advantageous in this circumstance. You can work together to resolve your disagreements and find a solution. Even if you are dissatisfied with the outcome, you should be willing to commit your teammates to aiding them in any manner they can.

When someone speaks through his teeth, in a perforating tone, or at an extreme volume, he is displaying hostility. Aggressive conduct involves being upset with someone, swinging your arms frantically, and being generally dissatisfied with how your message is portrayed. Excessive aggression, on the other hand, might result in a never-ending cycle of hostility, alienation, rage, and anger. The distinction between fear and respect is enormous. Rather of nurturing devotion, anger and fear tend to breed enmity in others. If others become aggressive toward you, you can employ tactics to avoid them.

1. Consult with a director about your case. Seeking the opinion of a qualified consultant or human resources manager may

help you handle the matter more swiftly if you believe someone is hostile toward you.
2. You can alter the emphasis, if necessary, by stating something like, "Why aren't we talking about something else?"
3. Recognize your emotions and discuss the situation with someone.
4. Someone may appear violent as a result of concern or tension over other issues. This is not uncommon. On occasion, other people's opinions have nothing to do with us but everything to do with them, and vice versa. Interacting with them will allow you to see if there is anything you can do to assist them in their attack.
5. Visit their social media accounts to learn more about them. Someone may assault you because they are unaware of who you are or believe you pose a threat to them. If you discover more about them, you'll be able to communicate with them.
6. Employ your emotional intelligence. Conduct an investigation to determine the reason of your dissatisfaction. Keep a tight check on them to ensure they don't become overly inflamed. Even though something cannot be taken away, something can be said and done about it.
7. If you feel embarrassed or threatened, stop talking and leave immediately. It is enough to just up and leave the room or structure.
8. Maintain a silent demeanor. Maintain your composure. If you get belligerent in an attempt to equalize with them, you risk worsening the conflict. If you lack self-control, you may suffer the same issues as others.

To appreciate one another, people must be self-assured. It's a diplomatic and effective form of communication. It exhibits your ability to collaborate with others to solve challenges. Confident communication includes respectful and direct communication. Whether you are silent or overly assertive, your delivery is more concentrated than your words. The success of every enterprise is predicated on trust, clarity, and control. It is critical not just to get the concept through, but also to do so effectively.

Working in business will bring you into contact with a big number of people. Some people are self-conscious and will not speak up for themselves; others are self-centered and will not allow others to speak for them. Some folks may even have a quick temper. If these folks grab control of either side of the room, there will be no room for good discourse. Half will speak, while the other half will remain silent. As a result, both creativity and productivity suffer.

Communication must be equitable and fair on all sides in order to be successful. One individual cannot communicate with another. You must have charisma, knowledge, emotional control, and the courage to speak up and defend your beliefs. Prepare yourself for the consequences of expressing your views. It doesn't look that things will keep going your way indefinitely. You must remember that you are confident in your ability to handle any circumstance that may arise.

Trust is required to stand alone in the face of hardship, fear, or challenges. A strong sense of self-assurance is necessary for achieving lofty goals and boosting overall satisfaction. Once you've piqued your audience's interest, prepare to give the complete message. Others are willing to listen to whatever you have to offer since you are focused on your objectives. If they answer with criticism, questions, or points of view, you must be prepared to carry on the conversation with the same level of confidence that you began with. In these situations, being direct allows you to respond effectively. Make your message brief and direct; this will allow you to get right to the point.

When someone disagrees with you or casts doubt on your opinions and beliefs, this is referred to as a challenge. Take this as a chance to defend yourself, not as a rejection. Your credibility will improve as a result. Consider these talks as chances to share your ideas with others. This keeps you from acting aggressively or defensively in social situations. You can feel hostile or defensive, as if your logic is faulty, and you might feel tempted to plug your throat. Examine conflicting evidence from your viewpoint point when it is presented to you. Explain in a calm and cool tone how and why you have a different point of view.

Directness and clarity improve others' abilities to speak with authority and effect. Make assured, however, that you comprehend the distinction between daring and disagreeable behavior. Being brave may get attention and appreciation; being ugly, on the other hand, may result in scorn. Your goal is for others to recognize and respect your point of view, as well as to take you seriously. You must be able to successfully explain your points of view in order to do so.

Businesses must be able to communicate and interact effectively in the workplace. It can be frightening to communicate one's thoughts and feelings in front of others. You may be concerned about the outcome or how others may see you. Being self-assured, on the other hand, ensures that you are regarded seriously. You don't waste time thinking about your life goals. You are capable of devoting a large quantity of time and mental energy to your remarks.

You will only have a limited time to make a proposal to a manager or someone in a position of power. You, on the other hand, have the ability to generate and manipulate data. Make a list of the three most significant aspects of your plan or proposal, as well as any potential benefits to other people or the company. You want to give them as much information as possible so that they will ask questions, which will allow you to expound on your idea and point of view. By being succinct, you prevent receiving a diluted version of your concept.

Using vulgarity and yelling will not get the same results as conversing. When sharing your thoughts and opinions, you can be both calm and assertive. If you are receptive and cooperative, you can initiate conversations that lead to solutions and better productivity. At work, self-control prevents you from tearing out your hair and wreaking chaos. Controlling your tone and body language enhances the result of workplace interactions.

Once you've provided them the information they require, they'll ask for more. This is your chance to learn about any items that were left out of the pitch. You have not only increased their knowledge, but you have also shown a willingness to learn more. Senior executives, in particular, are drawn to thought-provoking business themes. This means you'll be put through your paces on a frequent basis. These are the kinds of impediments that serve as catalysts for the emergence of fresh ideas and opportunities.

Chapter 23
What an Assertive Person is Like

A committed person accepts complete responsibility for his or her own activities. This is a serious assignment that should not be taken lightly because it entails full responsibility for your conduct. You can't blame someone else for every blunder you make. To be genuinely aggressive, you must accept complete accountability for whatever you do. On the other hand, how can we know when we aren't being forceful enough in our interactions with others? We've encountered the latter rather regularly as a result of our own personal flaws. However, we can see our aggressiveness in other circumstances.

People who lack assertiveness can give a variety of reasons. At times in our lives, we may feel compelled to apologize for nearly all of our activities. Have you ever accidentally spilled your coffee at your desk? After all, it wasn't your fault. You were alarmed by the sound of your children leaping in front of you. Is it possible that you took an incorrect turn on the road? It was once again the GPS's problem, not yours! We accept our apologies for the call you made. We frequently feel obligated to justify our refusal to join in particular activities, as well as to explain our misfortunes. If you don't want to go out with your friends on a Friday night, for example, you must explain why your party will take place instead. Individuals who are obstinately adamant do not require an explanation; they are merely stating that individuals do not like leaving things.

If you're touched by the question "but why?" a self-assured individual can use the broken record method and answer, "I just don't feel like that." The person in charge simply declines the invitation and goes about his or her business without explaining or justifying his or her decision. A confident person's goals are self-evident; he does not need to justify or justify his behavior. After all, it is ultimately up to each of us to make our own choices and create our own path in life. As independent thinkers, we should be able to make our own decisions without feeling forced to comply to others' expectations.

After your initial victory, you'll discover that a little patience and determination pays off. Whatever the barriers, if you know what you desire, you must pursue it with zeal. If someone tries to push you, simply remind them of your previously stated goals and objectives. Simply repeat yourself like a broken record, and they'll ultimately give up attempting to stop you.

A solid dedication to one's core values and convictions is the actual key of perseverance. Furthermore, if you are aware that you will be powerless to act, resist giving up your principles to fit in with others. Because patience is truly worth it when it is routinely exercised — or, for lack of a better term, consistently applied!

You're adamant about not being ineffectual, and you're not going down without a fight. Assertive people do not tolerate unnecessary conflict and are capable of rapidly and totally resolving the issue. If someone wants to debate and talk, the assertive person can avoid reinforcing his or her own assertiveness by being involved. Even if someone makes a low-cost attempt to damage your feelings, someone who is determined will be able to avoid becoming involved in the drama.

We recently addressed the idea of setting up a smokescreen to deceive an opponent. A smokescreen frequently verifies a chosen attacker's assertions in order to prevent being dragged down into the abyss. This technique denies an opponent what he can receive from you, prompting them to eventually give up and go on. Consider the following scenario: you've just completed mowing your front yard, and an annoying neighbor comes over to offer his unwelcome advice. This bully is weeping because he dislikes how short the grass is cut. "Hello there, pal! I couldn't help but notice your yard had lately been scalped! It's far too short. It's far too short." "Yes, that is a touch short," you can kindly point out. If the neighbor says, "You won't cut it that short anymore, right?" they may believe they have won the argument.

Instead of complying with his demands, the belligerent individual says, "I can see why you wouldn't want me to mow my lawn as short as you have." Instead of agreeing to cut the grass short, the assertive individual acknowledges that he understands the other person's point of view. He does not explicitly express that he would carry out the plan; instead, he simply recognizes that he understands what the other person said. However, if the neighbor wrongly believes that his comments have effectively bossed the man, he may become pushier and hiss at him. "To be honest, I'm relieved that you agree with me. I understand you believe that appears to be garbage," the self-assured man replies candidly. "Are you sure you're not going to do it again?"

Despite his assurance that the forceful would bow to his demands, the bully was eventually rebuffed. While everyone can maintain their calm and listen to others' concerns, they must eventually stand firm. People who want to fight will try to get you worked up to the point where you lose your ability to think clearly; but, if you can avoid this trap and demonstrate some knowledge and rationality, you will be regarded as someone who refuses to be cowed and who takes poison from these toxic people.

Chapter 24
When Nothing is Working

We're nearly finished with this book, and you've learned some of the most efficient methods to say no without offending others. Even if you haven't implemented everything yet, you may be noticing some of the benefits at work.

Furthermore, you might not get the desired outcomes, or you might not get any results at all. This does not preclude you from reaching your objective. Certain folks have a curve in both directions that is higher and lower than the Ferris wheel. For a week or two, you may have noticed huge improvements in your life, but then nothing happened for months. It will be challenging, but it will help you stay motivated.

If you're having problems analyzing the findings, keep track of how long you've been able to read the word without difficulty. It all begins when you're a child. Because of its frequent use, the word "no" is frequently the first thing that many young people think about. "No," they say as they approach the stove. They marked off some items from their month and wrote "No" next to them. If their children resist, their parents are forced to reprimand them. When a youngster refuses to go to bed, she is attempting to push her boundaries, yet she is reprimanded as a result of her activities.

Our parents have often warned us about the hazards of peer pressure throughout our youth and adulthood. However, the signals have grown muddled, and in order to be nice, we must respond favorably and assist others. It will take a long time in social situations for someone to be considered unfriendly to others. You're asked if you'd like to live for 20, 30, or 50 years. The answers to this question have shaped who you are now and changing your behaviors will take time. Before you become certain that nothing will work for you, tell yourself to be patient and to relax your self-criticism.

If you nod your head while reading the information, you may be unaware of the magnitude of your difficulties. Despite your experiences, you continue to feel that you are nice and that you want the best for others. It's possible that only after a comprehensive examination of the difficult reality would progress be accomplished. Your interpersonal relationships will be detrimental in the long run. Finally, your efforts to appease others benefit no one, and your relationships suffer as a result. You become nervous when you find yourself in a circumstance where you wish to say nothing but are unable to do so due to your progress toward your goal. You grow stressed as a result of a lack of personal time. You are physically and emotionally exhausted, which has an impact on your food, sexual life, sleep, and general mood. You risk tiredness, sexual experiences, and sadness.

We want you to be fearless throughout this activity. When speaking with customers in similar situations, it's likely that the issue is that they haven't been adequately focused on their goals and what they actually want to change. Perhaps the objectives are too broad and have not been broken down into manageable phases. Even while the aim of "I want to be happy" is a good place to start, keep in mind that this is a wish shared by everyone, not just you. Consider adjusting our goals.

As a result of being split down into three distinct reasons for achieving happiness, the goal may be divided into three more manageable categories:

The significance of objectives in our lives cannot be overstated. We're used to getting up, moving about, and sleeping when we don't have them. There is nothing that pushes us to grow or that we should strive for. If you believe your objectives were not properly prepared, return to this stage. Above all, keep your goals current. Maybe you've read this book in a week or a few months and seen that certain things have changed or that some of your short-term goals have been reached. Congratulations if this is the case! Take some time once a month to review your goals.

That is the most fortunate thing that has occurred to us. You did all possible to prepare for the situation, and you believe you did an excellent job, yet the other person expressed every emotion imaginable. You've been giggling and yelling, and you've been feeling a little ashamed. As a result, you've concluded that you never want to be in the same circumstance again, and that continuing to say yes is the easiest option.

One of the first thoughts that comes to mind is that this person's reaction is not a flaw and that you should not be embarrassed or irritated about it. Everything revolves around them, and they are the only ones who matter. Despite the fact that their behavior is unacceptable and should not be tolerated, you can only assume they had another personal issue that contributed to their out-of-control behavior. Make an attempt to irritate your tormentor. You have every right to be outraged at how you were treated, because no one has the authority to treat another person in this manner. Then, in order to be emotionally equipped to deal with your situation, you must find a way to express your wrath. You may not like it, but you must approach it again with your newly acquired aggressive qualities.

When you question the individual about his or her actions and let him or her to speak, he or she will recognize the ridiculousness of his or her viewpoint, and the two of you will reach an accord.

It may be tough to find the words to communicate exactly how you feel following a period of silence, and then hope that the other person understands. People who have trouble satisfying others have low emotional intelligence and a lack of understanding, use, and management of their own emotions. We are escaping conflict rather than defending ourselves and what we believe is correct in the situation. Increasing your emotional language may help you better understand your emotional feelings.

It is critical to select the correct words before beginning a conversation, whether you are communicating with others or expressing yourself. The word "sad," for example, will not suffice because it might mean many different things to different people. You may be feeling sorry for yourself as a result of bad weather, a broken nail, or the demise of your favorite sports team. Depression is a possibility if you feel humiliated, ashamed, or mocked.

Use an online thesaurus to try to expand your vocabulary. Fill in the blanks with the emotion you're experiencing and consider whether there are any other words that might better convey your emotions.

You're probably unhappy because of anything uncommon; gloomy implies you've lost something; unfortunate means you've made a mistake; or broken your heart because of a disagreement with a friend explains this predicament. Each of these sentences elicits a stronger emotional response than the word "sad." If you're having problems putting your sentiments into words, look up similar terminology to utilize while composing your speech.

You haven't done anything wrong; it's simply that folks aren't used to hearing "no," and persuading them may require a second attempt. Even if you eventually responded yes, the first time, the second time will be easier because you said no the first time. There's some excellent news to share. When you have the choice to say no to someone who has previously rejected your response, you must begin by reminding them that you have already had this conversation and will say something simple like, "I already said no because I was unavailable," or something similar. To please everyone, you must change your focus away from the original plan or idea and onto another option, such as postponing an event or changing your work schedule.

If individuals continue to disregard your no, you must become firmer and more confrontational while remaining on the correct side of the line. Reiterate your willingness to consider opposing points of view. If this doesn't work, leave the room, and don't return until the issue of the conversation is brought up again. Rather than becoming insulted or frustrated, consider it a friendly competition for a battle of wills. Some people become so consumed with saying no because they are afraid of being humiliated that it becomes hard for them to say yes, as if you put too much pressure on them to do so.

To avoid having to use the term explicitly, we employ phrases and statements that have no meaning in specific contexts. "Thank you, but I'm sorry, but I'm unable to," has the same result as saying no. You can confidently decline results that contain the word "no." If you don't want to be without the tumultuous experience of saying no, the advantages of saying no, such as freeing up time and avoiding overtime labor, will become clear.

Overcoming dysfunctional persons is a difficult learning curve, but keep in mind that the learning curve is upward, not downward. Things will only improve if you know exactly what you want and are willing to put up the effort required to obtain it. We always emphasize the need of patience and taking your time with the process, but there are times when you require results much faster than usual. We'll have a system in place for anyone who need outcomes in two weeks.

Chapter 25
Training your Mind to Become Assertive

We adopt certain behaviors and ways of living during our formative years that become second nature to us and that we take for granted. This is the time of year when we all reflect on our lives, express our frustrations, and plan long-term initiatives. These, on the other hand, do not appear to be permanent components of our identity.

We can almost surely learn not to do something if we've previously learned to do it. All it takes is a modest amount of conscious effort on our part to assist ourselves in changing. If you find yourself stuck in an unproductive and unbreakable thought and behavior cycle, you should read this chapter. Why? Because this is where you can learn how to rewire your brain.

What is the most effective approach to entirely alter your mind?

Consider the same ideas and emotions as if they were coming from someone else. Believe it or not, you have three and a half pounds of regulated gray matter in your skull. Indeed, research has demonstrated that the brain's shape can alter in response to our repeated ideas.

Self-limiting beliefs such as "I'm not good enough" or "This is too difficult" might result in the creation of specific neural pathways on the surface of our brain. These tunnels, which were a source of constant concern for us, served as mental highways of anxiety and uncertainty. This may appear exaggerated, but it is not. When we are overtaken with emotion or have an experience, specific neurons in our brain become active, building synaptic connections that allow us to recall the event. This phenomenon is known as "neuroplasticity." This is the phenomenon I alluded to earlier.

Consider the following scenario: we are delivering a public speech that goes disastrously wrong, and some neurons fire because of the event. If we don't strive to manage our negative ideas, the same neurons will activate the next time we speak, or even before we try, implying that making public comments is harmful for our health and just creates suffering.

Even public opinion, if it persists, will frighten you since the same neurons fire and the brain forecasts the same horrifying future as before. Isn't that a touch too tempting? However, there is some good news: we can modify it at the same rate as our thought patterns change.

While this is frequently the case, it is not always easy to keep our information up to date. Our mental status quo is so ingrained in our daily lives and experiences that it has the potential to become our entire identity. For a moment, imagine that a person has been timid and shy for a long period. Their shyness and timidity may appear to be ingrained characteristics. Individuals may even make public statements "Oh, he (or she) is so quiet! They're exactly as they should be!"

Furthermore, if such features are strongly related to one's identity, eliminating undesirable ideas may be challenging. People who are constantly irritated by the world can be described similarly. They are widely awaited all throughout the world, and they are always willing to hear public concerns or other forms of concern.

Even this heinous individual, no matter how bad things appear to be, could be persuaded by some unique — and possibly commendable — character traits. People who are chronically dissatisfied and consider themselves as heroic underdogs, as well as campaigners who are frequently mistaken but unwavering in their pursuit of justice, are examples. While such a self-perception is illogical, believing that one is a champion in one's own world of suffering and struggle can become a permanent part of one's reality.

And if someone were to demonstrate that the conditions were not as horrible as they had been made out to be, that individual would be pushed into a complete identity crisis. This is the danger of becoming overly engaged in such thoughts and beliefs over time.

Regardless of how difficult these problems are, concerted effort can produce visible and consistent results. If you want to stay on your current route, diverting your focus away from the outer world and all its apparent shortcomings will not help you break free from your current rut. After doing an honest self-analysis, you may be able to begin the process of reprogramming your brain.

For many years, clinical specialists have universally recognized CBT, or cognitive behavioral treatment, as having considerable benefits. Cognitive behavioral therapy (CBT) aims to improve a person's behavior in life by changing the thoughts that flow through his or her head on a regular basis. As previously mentioned in this book, we are all constantly thinking, even if we aren't aware of it. Our ideas are automatic, and they may be communicated so silently that we are unaware we are doing so.

As our understanding of our own thoughts and experiences expands, we will be able to discriminate between well-founded and ill-founded concepts. The "BLUE model" was deemed effective by cognitive behavioral therapy (CBT) participants. The BLUE model outlines the processes required to complete a transformation. BLUE is a color that acts as a reminder of the potentially harmful cycles we may find ourselves in.

Keep a tight eye on your goals.

Individuals who are self-confident must be aware of their environment. This necessitates the establishment of attainable goals. Instead of being unrealistic, one's aims should be practical. Almost any fitness professional will tell you that beginning slowly is preferable to beginning quickly.

Rather than starving yourself and exercising for several hours at a time, the ideal course of action is to just cut back on needless calories and go for a late-night walk. After you've fulfilled your primary targets, you can progress to more difficult and remarkable goals in the future. To prevent getting too far ahead of yourself and never reaching your goals, keep your objectives within striking distance of your current location.

Because I was saddled with significant student debt after graduation, I had to learn how to prioritize my own aspirations. Many recent grads are concerned, so they attempt to pay more than they can, eventually falling behind on their payments. I was lucky to be accepted into a program that will allow me to achieve my goals.

They went over everything with me, including how I could stay on track and pay off my debt by making a fixed monthly payment. My loans could be completely canceled if I maintain excellent health and contribute to my community during the period. I'm happy to announce that these goals have been nearly totally met.

It merely depicts the possibility of achieving attainable goals. Exaggeration is unneeded; simply make the best of the situation. Maintain a firm grasp on your dreams, and you will be able to attain all your goals with enough effort and determination. All that remains is for you to select an appropriate objective and begin working toward it.

At all costs, negative self-talk must be avoided.

Do you have a negative outlook? Do you have a negative outlook? I understand your amazement at hearing this because your ears are constantly talking to each other. All the trivialities of daily life are constantly dissected and scrutinized in the dungeons of your mind. The bulk of us are entirely unaware that we are engaging in this activity, as though it is ingrained into our DNA. It may seem strange to simply declare that we can hear our own thoughts. It is, however, correct—and the proof is straightforward.

As a result, until you read these words out, you will only be able to "hear" your own ideas by softly repeating them to yourself in your head. It is still unknown what process permits us to "hear" without utilizing our ears and instead relying on our inner consciousness.

We are all performing this responsibility 24 hours a day, seven days a week, whether we are conscious of it or not. Unfortunately, negative self-talk is all too common for many of us. Consider the following example: You've just finished delivering a presentation in front of your peers, and you're thinking to yourself, "Oh, my God, this is utterly horrible!" This, my friends, is a habit of negative self-talk. It should also be outlawed.

Whenever you have a negative thought, attempt to answer with a positive phrase. Consider the following scenario: You're getting ready to give a big speech and were concerned about what you'd say the night before. "Oh, my God, I'm going to be terrified up there." You're contemplating something. Discuss your thoughts with someone else after you've formed an opinion.

Make a mental note of it to remind yourself later "I'm not going to be fazed at all. I'm going to keep my cool, and I'm going to keep my cool throughout! It's going to be fantastic!" It may appear amusing at first, but believe it or not, it works. As you have more positive feelings about an experience, your chances of having a positive outcome grow. Positive self-fulfillment is a reality in the same way that negative self-fulfilling prophesies are. Assume that everything is fine in your life. Believe in your ability and yourself to triumph in this situation. Keep negative thoughts to a minimum—and succeed!

Self-assured yet not arrogant

The number of citations for this publication compels trust. Because, while some self-confidence is beneficial, being overconfident in one's own talents and displaying what others may refer to as "cockiness" is not.

On its own, the sentence looks to be self-explanatory. Knowing what to do and doing it is a component of being brave and having trust. When someone is considered arrogant, they are perceived as a nasty, obnoxious bully. Who wants that information made public in the first place? The arrogant bully must constantly overlap his hand and exert tremendous effort to keep power through his bluster, whereas confident people may easily show respect.

It needs good art to foster trust and dispel hubris. Confidence should not be imposed just for the sake of imposing it. Others will trust you because you believe in yourself and your objective. If you play the guitar and believe you have what it takes to become the next Jimi Hendrix, believe in yourself and trust that your confidence will come across as genuine rather than arrogant.

Jimi Hendrix is a fantastic illustration of this, since he was himself a tremendous example. In contrast, Jimi was always humble about it, bringing up other guitarists on the spot and insinuating that they could be better than him.

Despite his persistent downplaying of his abilities, Jimi Hendrix was aware of his guitar prowess. To achieve anything, we set our minds to, we all need a fundamental amount of humble self-confidence.

Act as if you're successful—fake it until you make it!

Despite its absurdity, that sentence contains significant truths, as is often the case with ancient words of wisdom. While the term "faking" may not excite you, it is an effective method of making it appear as if you are not in the current situation.

You are confident in your ability to put your best foot forward and travel as far as possible throughout the day, even if you are not quite there yet. In other words, despite your lack of confidence in yourself, you project a confident manner. Something happens after a while that leads you to feel you're a part of a scripted routine.

Conclusion

Personal affirmation is not a miraculous talent that is conferred on some people but not on others. Even if you believe you lack confidence, putting the strategies in this book to use will swiftly convert you into a more confident version of yourself.

I hope that this work has demonstrated the validity of this claim. We looked at some of the most effective tactics for protecting your rights while remaining calm and respectful to others in this book. After example, an assertive communicator is not the same as an aggressive communicator. While no one admires a bully, everyone admires someone who can express themselves peacefully while simultaneously attempting to comprehend the perspectives of others.

Assertiveness is essential in this situation. When so many of us find ourselves in contentious and stressful situations, the ability to quietly sort things out and communicate them with others is vital. However, as this book has demonstrated, a large portion of our ability to establish ourselves and our values is contingent on our first understanding of who we are as individuals.

To effectively explain our fundamental values and points of view to others, we must keep them in mind at all times. Because how can we expect others to understand what is essential to us if we don't understand ourselves? We can't expect everyone to be diligent readers who pick up on our clues. To thrive, we must be direct and confident about who we are as individuals and what we expect of others around us.

This book provides tried-and-true techniques. Don't be afraid to put what you've learned to use right away. It's your life, and only you can determine how you want to live it.

Asserting one's rights is a deliberate effort refined through years of trial and error, not a mystical, miraculous technique. Building oneself is a constant process, not a one-time event that happens overnight. If you've finished this book and understood how to finish it, you've only begun your journey along a new and determined road!

www.ingramcontent.com/pod-product-compliance
Lightning Source LLC
Chambersburg PA
CBHW050234120526
44590CB00016B/2081